High moments of student unrest – the May 1968 events in Paris, the violent clashes in Rome and West Berlin – are reported exhaustively in the press and on television. But the treatment seems often superficial and the tone sometimes patronizing: Starry-eyed students storming Heaven.

The Student Revolt puts the record straight. As the student leaders answer their interrogators, directly and without rhetoric, the words 'student' and 'young' seem to become increasingly irrelevant. As Cohn-Bendit and Geismer and the others say their say, one begins to hear the *total* troubled voice of our consumer-oriented society.

The Student Revolt is an uncomfortable experience. It is also a salutary one.

The
Student Revolt

The Activists Speak

compiled by Hervé Bourges
translated by B. R. Brewster

A Panther Book

The Student Revolt
A Panther Book

First published in Great Britain
by Jonathan Cape Limited 1968

Panther edition published 1968

Translated from the French
La Révolte Etudiante

Copyright © Editions du Seuil
Translation copyright ©
Jonathan Cape Limited and
Hill & Wang Inc 1968

*Printed in Great Britain by Cox & Wyman Ltd.,
London, Reading and Fakenham, and published
by Panther Books Ltd.,
3 Upper James Street, London, W.1*

Contents

The Student Revolt

ONE

Foreword

LYRICAL ILLUSION, nostalgia and adventurism, manipulation. These are the terms in which the right has exorcized the revolutionary demons now that the May danger is over; they are too virulent to be examined face to face. Besides, it is now free, in the name of France's indomitable spirit, and by virtue of an enlightened nationalism, to draw glory from this people, 'light, brilliant ... always consistent with itself, even in its sudden reversals'.

On the left, however, exploitation, canalization, reinflation; counting chickens, too.

And once more the procession of conformisms and calculations of every kind is assembled around the old slogans. The whole social *tartuferie*, caught for a moment in the trap of naked truth, would rather integrate the challenge than try to understand it.

Yesterday, everyone spoke of the necessity for university reform. The left accused the Gaullist regime of doing nothing in ten years, the better to mask its own impotence. The government shook its rattle, the Fouchet reforms,[1] and machinated

---

[1] Fouchet Plan: A plan for the university system to modernize the courses and to rationalize the production of students according to the needs of the French economy. It is therefore based on intense specialization

to destroy UNEF,[1] as it refused to be taken in. Part of the teaching body slumbered in intellectual sloth, lack of imagination, and an insistence on changing nothing that might force it to overthrow its habits of thought and its patterns of work.

Then came the days of wrath. Nanterre[2] was aflame, the Sorbonne an example, and the whole framework of the bourgeois university shook. The established order collapsed before the barricades. The revolt spread to the factories. The State seemed to dissolve. Society was cracking up.

Nonplussed for a moment, the President-General rose up to defy the 'chaos'. The number of his followers swelled with all the survivors of this terrible nightmare. And life resumed. Despite some recalcitrance, the workers little by little returned to the factories, the employees to the offices, the citizens to the ballot-boxes. Things returned to normal, for, if a general is made to command, so is an opposition to be divided, workers to work, and citizens to elect.

And are not students made to study? Then why are they dawdling like this? Why this unwillingness to accept the rules of the game, this refusal to see their reforms granted them, this desire to overthrow a society that does not want to be overthrown?

They do not believe in substitute solutions. The old order has grown old. Nothing will restore it, in the university at any rate. They will sooner or later have to be granted a total re-

and thus provides the basis for the social and technological divisions of society. The Plan Fouchet is the mirror image in the university of the Fifth Plan (see p. 68).

[1] A list of abbreviations appears on p. 141.

[2] Nanterre: a recently erected and oppressively designed, unfinished campus outside Paris, isolated amongst the neighbouring slums. The students are socially divided between those who come from the wealthy quarters of Paris and those who are forced to live on the campus. It was here that the student uprising began.

form of the structure, on the basis of autonomy and joint control. But since the university has no frontiers, since it is directly at grips with society, since, for better or worse, a unity of students and workers was achieved, revolutionary action cannot be confined to a domain reserved for the intelligentsia. Every political phenomenon today is intensified by mass effect and contagion. The social process as a whole has been opened up.

If so, it is no longer a question of whether the revolution can be achieved and whether the majority wants it, but when and in what form it will take place. What revolution? First of all, the economic revolution. Let sceptical spirits smile at the incredible naivety of the most committed students who have attacked the citadel of so-called advanced capitalism only to enter on the same quest as so many of their elders, the quest for a true socialism. Then the revolution in political life. All the cards were false, so the students have rejected the parliamentary game and all forms of democracy, classical or modern. A new type of intervention has now emerged, outside the traditional organizations. Finally, a revolution in social and cultural relations: no doubt imagination will have its hands full discovering how to make men both free and more in solidarity with one another.

Thus, schematically, the meaning of a crisis whose repercussions promise to be vast: the crazy impetus of the *journées* of May, the brutal spontaneity and the immense de-repression manifested are not a game, they signify the failure of a particular form of civilization, and call for a total renaissance. Can this be achieved in the control of those who are responsible for it, or, once 'anarchy' has been crushed, must we wait long years for the re-emergence, perhaps more violent, of revolutionary faith?

At present, more dangerous than ever, the dialogue of the deaf between the tenants of the established order and those 'few chimerical spirits' who have rejected the fallacious promises of growth and efficiency as a kind of conditional happiness, in the name of an intense need for freedom, goes on. 'All power to the imagination!' may be a bad bedfellow for economic law. But what a challenge to mental torpor, to prejudice, to ideological sclerosis, to bureaucracy! Should confused ideas, diversity of organizations and initials, and utopian perspectives be pretexts for the rejection of a fruitful challenge? Should anathemas be cast on the Latin Quarter, swept as it is by a tonic gale? Should we refuse to hear this novel language?

A few actors in this drama today have familiar names and faces. Their actuality has made them reluctantly famous. Alain Geismar, Jacques Sauvageot, Daniel Cohn-Bendit have agreed time and time again to explain their attitudes and their commitments. It will be objected that they are not necessarily representative of students and teachers. It is true, many have shared the experience of the *journées* of May, vaguely aware of what they meant, dissolving their contradictions in solidary action. Then, returning to the shadows, they have devoted themselves to the more arid but creative tasks of reflection, discussion and elaboration in their respective faculties and schools. Their revolt is revealing in itself, even if its content has not yet been articulated. Its fantastic dynamism has sufficiently affected the country's destiny for it to be legitimate to interrogate those to whom it has given its confidence.

Three leaders: two students under twenty-five, one teacher under thirty. Along with a few others, these three initiated the common action of the National Union of French Students (UNEF), the March 22nd Movement,[1] and the National Union

[1] March 22nd Movement: A movement, born in Nanterre, which gathered militants, both workers and students, of different viewpoints in a specific programme of action. There is no leadership, no membership;

of Higher Education (SNESup).

The 'March 22nd' militants opened the breach at Nanterre. Few in number but determined, disorderly in discussion and organized in action, they do not regard themselves as representing the students as a whole, but as constituting a kind of vanguard. Their programme? They have none, if by a programme you mean a collection of texts printed on shiny paper and suitably arranged. Their aim is nothing less than a total reform of the university, its structure, its spirit and its aims, and the transformation of bourgeois society.

A vast project whose application begins with a permanent challenge to the teachers, the authorities, the monopolies and imperialism – in a word, to everything in France or the world that they feel has to be opposed, fought and overthrown. If they want revolution, they do not propose to lead it through a party. The enemy is capitalist society; the hindrance is bureaucratic organization. What is their strategy? To be present everywhere, to invent forms of action adapted to the circumstances: a flexible formula suitable for a small number, and ensuring the success of particular interventions.

Officially the movement has no leadership. Various tendencies coexist within it. But still, a dozen militants with no special prerogatives do stand out, no doubt because of their energy, their tactical sense and their understanding of situations. Daniel Cohn-Bendit is among them. Small and compact, with red hair (though it might just as well be black if disguise is called for) and astonishingly clear blue eyes, Daniel Cohn-Bendit has been the Robin Hood of the feverish *journées* of May. Flexible and determined, uniting a taste for danger and forethought, he is a man of action, a conscious anarchist, not an adventurer. His ascendency is due to his

everyone is responsible for himself and for the movement. It started by maintaining that to transform the university system, society itself must be transformed, which can only happen through the working class.

exceptional leader's temperament. By turns he shows himself and disappears, urges on or calms down. If he has a feeling for striking expressions, he does not always avoid a verbal extremism that discredits him in the eyes of the public.

Promoted to the headlines by the partisan bourgeois press who have played on his origins and his nationality for sensational purposes, Cohn-Bendit has used the platform offered him to explain the actions of the organization he belongs to and to initiate the stupefied Frenchman into the process unleashed by the March 22nd Movement: a hundred students soon joined by tens of thousands more, united against repression, who dragged the whole of society into the maelstrom.

There is one 'institution' among the allies, a sign of their seriousness. In the tiny offices at 28 rue Monsieur-le-Prince, on the first floor of an old Latin Quarter block, a strange disorder reigns; leaflets, papers, union officials, telephone bells, waiting journalists, nervous teachers, for a fortnight the SNESup premises were the headquarters of the rebellion and its communications centre. Calm amid the tumult, plump-cheeked, tranquil Alain Geismar, General Secretary of SNESup, betrays nothing suggesting revolutionary torment. At first welcoming and fraternal, he admitted later to fatigue, due to his numerous responsibilities.

Aware of the importance of the part he was playing, he did not hesitate to throw his union into the fight. Formed in union and political activity, he has a strong personality and, as a good Marxist, a taste for dialectic. An enemy of all bureaucracy, and very critical of the French Communist Party (PCF), he has avoided the rigid dogmatism of the bureaucrat. He has always defended a hard line in the union, calling for a radical transformation of the university and opposing the conservatism of the teaching body. This is enough to show that he was not caught off his guard by the struggle. Nor was he much surprised by the attitude of the PCF and the General Confederation of Labour (CGT) to the student initiative, for he is familiar with the strict discipline of Communist Party militants, who are partisans of a 'united front' of all academics against the government.

Self-confident and strong-willed, he was not afraid to take on responsibilities alone, supported rather than surrounded by the SNESup executive. The support he brought to the students decisively affected the course of events. Slanderers suggest that he would even commit UNEF without consulting it. A sincere militant, but before all else an experienced politician, he registered and utilized every clumsy move on the authorities' part, without, however, ever despising dialogue. Like Sauvageot and Cohn-Bendit, he tried to restrict the confrontation, preferring spectacular demonstrations to unleashed violence.

Soon, assessing the scope of the struggle as going well beyond the union context, and wishing to ensure himself more freedom of movement, he resigned from his office as General Secretary (the post has since become a group responsibility) so that while remaining a member of the National Executive he could devote himself to political action, becoming – only the CGT is committed to this assessment – 'a specialist in provocation'.

UNEF, whose action is admitted to have been the most decisive, is no newcomer to the political scene; long divided into 'corporatists' and 'unionists', with the latter first in a majority and then in a minority, it has been attacked by the successive governments of the Fourth Republic and even by those of the Fifth, particularly for its stand in favour of Algerian independence. Since 1961 it has received the hardest knocks: the creation at government initiative of a rival union, the FNEF, and the removal of its subsidies. So it is not without

15

irony that during the crisis its officials were the recipients of pressing advances from the government, which wanted the students to file peacefully by under the control of a movement whose representativeness it had always disputed.

As conflict succeeded conflict, its last President finally resigned, and the deeply divided general meeting was unable to replace him. In these conditions, the Vice-President, Jacques Sauvageot, emerged to lead the students into battle, with authority and intelligence. Experienced in union activity, he takes account of the reactions at the base, and respects the collectivity of decisions.

SNESup, UNEF and the March 22nd Movement present a united front to the brutality of the repression. The action that welds them together is more important than the organizational modalities that separate them. Differences in style and assessment do not reduce the common depth of their demands.

They are agreed in demanding 'student power', conceived as the power to challenge and control, and university autonomy, that is, structural reforms allowing a redefinition of the relations between students and teachers on the one hand, and between university and government on the other. These are the basic demands for SNESup and UNEF, but the March 22nd Movement does not want to restrict itself to purely student demands. 'We are a political movement, not a student movement' is a favourite saying of its militants; they give top priority to workers' action.

Their global analyses come together again when they regard the present reform of education as the instrument of a policy of efficiency, aimed essentially at the creation of specialized personnel adapted to new production techniques. Knowledge then has an oppressive character, integrating its 'beneficiaries' into society as labour-power, like the rest of the workers, or as technocratic cadres to ensure the cohesion of the economic and social system. Hence the students' denunciation of capitalist structures and of the authorities that consolidate them, hence their defiance of the one and rejection of the other in opposition to the parliamentary system. This last challenge is the more far-reaching. Its language is more novel, and more concrete, too. So they are pitiless towards bourgeois democracy and its political personnel, even the members of the opposition.

No one finds grace in the eyes of Geismar or the March 22nd Movement, not even Mendès-France – whom the former regards as 'the bourgeoisie's last chance', while Sauvageot and many students recognize his worth, regarding him as the sole leader of the parliamentary left to have understood the revolutionary nature of the student demands.

Even less illusions about the PCF; it has displaced the struggle from its true terrain, the streets and the factories, by calling for general elections; it dreams of a respectable succession in the democratic temple, the Palais Bourbon. Less still about the CGT, which mystifies the workers by spreading empty formulae and encloses them in the cramped and demagogic perspective of material demands.

That is why it is essential to go directly to the working class, to make contact with the base, to show the workers that their problems are not qualitatively different from those of the students. The long marches from Paris to Boulogne-Billancourt and the fraternization were not as resounding as had been hoped? Why be surprised? Years of ignorance and compartmentalization separate the two universes. But already, beyond the naivety, the misunderstandings and the disillusionment, a dialogue has been established, a unity clumsily achieved, on common themes: direct action, occupation, workers' control. This will be tomorrow's ferment, it initiates ineluctable transformations.

For Geismar, Sauvageot and the militants of the March 22nd Movement, the truth of today and tomorrow is to be found precisely in joint action in factory and university, in the establishment of workers' power and student power, the complementary promises of a new, decentralized, socialist society. Hence the role that devolves on all the action committees and liaison committees, hence also the refusal to let them be confiscated by professional politicians.

As we can see, capitalism and the contradictions it produces in the social order, the impasses of politics and the bureaucratism of the organizations, are fought on the basis of a critical analysis of the university milieu, and within this milieu first of all, with a clear consciousness that these struggles have only a symbolic value unless they are extended by those of the workers. On this point of the analysis, too, the leaders of all the tendencies agree; they may be able to pose the question of power at their own level, but they will not make the revolution on their own. There can be no question of dissociating the movement in the universities from its context.

From this point, strictly political commitments may be more or less far-reaching in their different directions, but they must be conceived in terms of priorities and in original forms, even in France, with an acute awareness that this battle is the best way to unite with anti-imperialist struggles everywhere, the best way to oppose the detour of neo-colonialism, to support the resolute struggles of the Vietnamese, Palestinian and Latin-American peoples, and finally to witness to a desire shared today in a number of Eastern countries for the reconciliation of socialism and freedom.

This international openness, which is not in contradiction with the declared intention to fight in a limited terrain, is demonstrated by the generous cosmopolitanism of the Sorbonne, open to all the hopes of the Third World, by the blending in posters and unexpected meetings of ethnic and political minorities, by the inevitable tensions that this effervescence generates and the unambiguous attitude of the officials – as shown, for example, in the intervention of the Sorbonne Occupation Committee in defence of the right of *El Fatah* militants to express their views on the university's walls as much as anyone else.

Utopia, or tomorrow's reality? The last twitches of a suffocating civilization, or man's last chance? Certainly a vanguard struggle; the resistances still to be overcome are strong ones, the perspectives remote, the radical reforms demanded still inaccessible. But so long as the revolutionary impulse feeds a creative challenge, the shocks suffered by society will be salutary ones, forcing it into motion. But the most lucid do not conceal the gap that separates their action from its conclusion. If we can avoid revolution, we shall not avoid spiritual insurrection.

Paris
June 1st, 1968   HERVÉ BOURGES

Three
Interviews

The three interviews that follow were recorded between May 20th and June 1st, and have been transcribed more or less as they were given for the sake of accuracy.

TWO

Jacques Sauvageot
UNEF

*To initiate a permanent
challenge by way of
student power*

HERVÉ BOURGES: Were you surprised by the suddenness and
extent of the student mobilization?

JACQUES SAUVAGEOT: The student revolt was inevitable
and foreseeable. An analysis of the university situation in
France and abroad, and of the struggles that have broken out
in Italy and Germany, for example, would have shown that.
The university plays a larger and larger part in society, and in
the economy in particular. It has a monopoly in the intellectual
training and the research that strictly condition any economic
development today. This means that the whole economic
system must take more and more account of the university,
and it must have a more and more direct influence over it. The
result is that in the capitalist system, universities are more and
more subordinate to the criteria of a capitalist society.

Students are expected to have a certain critical intelligence,
while their studies are such that they are not allowed to exercise it. On the other hand, they realize that in a few years' time
they will not be able to find a part to play in society that
corresponds to their training. This dual phenomenon is, I
believe, the basic cause of their revolution. In the immediate
future, the most important monopoly in every society will be

the monopoly of education, for economic development depends on it. And in every country, and not just in capitalist ones, the students are determined to reject any ideological subjection.

With this background of growing unrest, an awareness that the authorities were going to inaugurate an extremely strict selection next session made us think that there would then be a brutal explosion. So the leaders of the various groups, including UNEF, prepared themselves to organize this movement when next session began.

Why did the movement explode in May? We should note that many things contribute towards the release of a student movement, to its immediate origin, that are outside the university itself. In Germany, for example, it was the problem of Vietnam. In Italy it was even more confused: the movement began in Rome when, one morning, students gave out leaflets calling for a Vietnam demonstration, and brought police repression down on to themselves. But the movement's detonation comes after a preparatory phase. Students – for example, in Western Germany at the University of Berlin, in Italy, in Nanterre – were induced to examine a number of problems, notably the problem of the content and aims of their education, usually brought into question by the examinations. Besides, this is the moment when governments find a pretext to intervene and brutally to repress the students' struggles.

Although this level of consciousness had not been reached in France, the situation had been deteriorating for some time. UNEF, for example, had been more active than in the previous year, with national campaigns[1] – campaigns which were not

[1] In December against selection next session, against the statutes, and for a radical transformation of the university; in February for campus freedom, and later in solidarity with the Vietnamese people; and in March once again against selection and for campus freedom.

unsuccessful – and a whole series of demonstrations[1] that, despite everything, involved more students than in previous years. The Gaullist government was strong enough to ensure the strict application of its line, limiting violent intervention; the frequent participation of students in movements in support of the liberation of the peoples of the Third World was tolerated by the French government because it did not feel itself to be essentially threatened by such actions. In this its attitude contrasted markedly with that of other European governments. Such Social-Democratic or openly reactionary governments, with much closer links to American imperialism, had to react more intransigently and more rapidly. Personally, I think that if we had had a Social-Democratic government, it would have acted against the students much earlier, for it would have been caught between its desire to represent the mass of the population, the students and workers, and the pursuit of an objectively capitalist policy. It seems to me that the Gaullist government put off the moment of its intervention as long as possible.

It was not the closing of the Nanterre faculty that aroused the students as a whole, but its direct repercussion, the intervention of the police at the Sorbonne during a meeting we held there the next day to widen the struggle. Besides, I believe that the government was bound to intervene sooner or later, caught as it was between its desire to avoid a clash and its fear that it would be overtaken by any freedoms it unwillingly conceded. So it had to react or let everything slide. It chose to act at the Sorbonne.

[1] February 21st: solidarity with the Vietnamese people;
  March 14th: national day of action;
  March 28th: selection and university building;
  second fortnight of April: solidarity, twice, with German students and with the Greek people.

H.B.: Did Vietnam and the Vietnam Committees play any direct part in all this?

J.S.: Not, I think, in the student milieu; on the other hand, in the schools the Vietnam Committees were initially very important. Many groups formed around militants from the Vietnam Committees. If we must reveal the influences, I should say that Dutschke's attempted assassination could be added to the action of the Vietnam Committees, the Italian revolt, the events in Greece and the campus movement that prefigured the general university movement, with students occupying the buildings and defying the internal regulations.

So I do believe that events outside found an echo here in France. Besides, student movements are inevitably international, and the French movement is sensitive to anything that happens in any university anywhere in the world.

But if we compare the French situation to the situation in other countries, we must add another element which is unique to the French student movement: the existence within the university of an important fringe of politicized students, and, above all, of a union, or if you prefer it, a student organization – UNEF – which is highly politicized.

The fact that many militants belong to very different movements was initially a hindrance to ours; this diversity and the inter-group rivalries that resulted from it acted as a brake on the movement. Thus UNEF, led by highly politicized elements, found itself to some extent cut off from the mass of students, or, at least, well ahead of them. This too might initially have been an element of weakness. But once the movement had been unleashed, the vanguard position held by individuals, groups and organizations such as UNEF, helped it to develop much more rapidly.

H.B.: Did Nanterre serve as a pilot project?

J.S.: Perhaps. I say 'perhaps' because it was a long time before anyone realized what was happening at Nanterre, for the press gave a distorted interpretation of it, stressing only the picturesque elements. Even at our level, there was little grasp of the importance of the work achieved there in the commissions, particularly those devoted to the content of education and to the examinations. We were so ill-informed that, until I had a conversation with Cohn-Bendit when we were arrested together by the police, I was unaware of the positive action achieved at Nanterre.

H.B.: Before the events UNEF was divided and regarded as weak. How is it today?

J.S.: UNEF has emerged from the events with an increased student audience. We have not resolved our organizational problems, but UNEF's authority has been extended and consolidated.

H.B.: But what is UNEF? What did it represent during all these events?

J.S.: For many people UNEF may only seem to be a handful of individuals. During the movement, UNEF was in fact a megaphone, defining a number of aims, advancing a number of propositions, as for example during the demonstrations. It also acted as a co-ordinating centre. The fact that the movement grew in the provinces was due to UNEF action.

H.B.: Do you really work as a team? Aren't you afraid that you may have lapsed into a personality cult?

J.S.: The press needs an official spokesman, a 'figurehead', but in reality we do work as a team, and anyway we are trying more and more to express ourselves in collective statements. In Paris, at any rate, we have a team; this team has close contact with the militants in the provinces, whom we have recently asked to come to the national executive so that we could examine together the decisions that we have to take. The role of the provinces is very important. When certain forms of action, for example, mass demonstrations, are forbidden us in Paris, the provinces can allow us to respond.

H.B.: Will you now consolidate the movement's organization, or would you rather let it develop spontaneously?

J.S.: The two things are not incompatible. It is possible both to let the base express itself and to attempt to structure the movement. In a leaflet which we have recently issued we call for the creation of student power, whether this goes to the union or to the strike committee. What is important today is to develop the struggle, according to proposals which the students themselves decide on. If the UNEF section refuses to fight in a certain locality, whereas student committees are disposed for action, then we recognize the latter.

The most urgent problems don't seem to me to be organizational ones. It would be dangerous to centralize and coordinate too quickly and sharply, particularly if this were to restrict the spontaneity which has been the movement's strength.

H.B.: Aren't you afraid you might be outflanked?

J.S.: That is a false problem. We have always acted according to what students were thinking. Of course, we have made mistakes, and we have publicly admitted them, notably on the famous Wednesday when we called students to the Sorbonne and then had to disperse them, and then again when we proposed to deal with trade-union organizations as apparatus to apparatus. The problem is not to know whether you are going to be outflanked, but by whom, and on what basis.

H.B.: You have said several times that you do not regard the government as a 'valid interlocutor'. Have you tried to make contact with it?

J.S.: Our position is clear. For more than a year, UNEF has refused to participate in the *Conseil national des œuvres*.[1] We maintained this position even in February, although we had enough information about the situation in the *Cités Universitaires* to know that we were in a position of strength. We have known for a long time that it is useless to talk to the government. There is only one thing that counts, the balance of forces; what has just happened has shown that.

We might have entered into discussions on the aims we had at the beginning of the events: release and amnesty for the demonstrators, police withdrawal, faculty reopening. But what produced the result was action; not that we succeeded by force, but that we won politically; the population was with us. That is what forced the government to give way. Discussions would have been useless. The problem has not changed.

We have never had any relations with the government, even when it contacted us by radio. We shall continue in this path. The platform we are going to elaborate will be submitted to the students for approval. When they have adopted it, we shall make it known. The government may accept part of it,

[1] Conseil National des Œuvres: A commission concerned with government direction of university facilities, i.e. restaurants, halls of residence, etc. Before 1963 it was co-managed by the students and the government; but now it is made up as follows: one-third are personalities nominated by the Minister of Education; one-third are university staff; and one-third are students.

and reject the rest. We shall continue the struggle for what has not been accepted.

H.B.: Will you resort to your idea of convening a States General to work out your platform?

J.S.: It is an interesting idea so long as the participants have precise mandates. Once we have worked out our platform and it has been discussed in the various universities, students as a whole would be able to come together to vote with a full knowledge of the case.

H.B.: Do you accept the widespread notion that the government attempted to promote UNEF, to strengthen you, to secure you from the 'extremists'? Do you think that such an operation was really mounted?

J.S.: I do think that it might have been part of the government's plans; it has been trying for some time to divide the students into leaders and led. Indeed, at one time it did try to play the 'UNEF is a serious organization' card, suggesting that we were more responsible than the others. The purpose behind this was not to open a dialogue or negotiations, but to sow discord among the students. To avoid this trap, we have always demonstrated our solidarity with other student movements and refused to open a dialogue with the government, which has few illusions about our desire to negotiate, anyway.

H.B.: If the government were to propose certain reforms, do you think that the student milieu would stick to its refusal to negotiate?

J.S.: The student milieu must preserve its unity so that cohesion will be maintained in the face of the government's manoeuvres. As for us, our position is clear: no negotiation with the government.

H.B.: If a government of the left is formed soon, will your demands for university reform take the same form as they do today?

J.S.: Your question is a false one. As far as I am concerned, a 'left' government means nothing. Those who might be at the head of a so-called government of the left have not, I think, shown as yet that they would be capable of dealing with the situation.

Neither Mitterrand nor Waldeck-Rochet could have found a solution during the movement. We have long felt that parliamentary debates were boring. Besides, when students passed by the Chamber of Deputies during their demonstrations, they none of them paid it the slightest attention. On the other hand, the problems posed by the workers produced a motion of censure: the result was the *coup de grâce* given to Mitterrand and Waldeck-Rochet.[1]

If Mendès-France has retained a certain audience, it is because he did not associate himself with this farce: whatever judgment I may have of him and his political future in other respects, and though he is not regarded as a valid interlocutor by some highly politicized students, others still favour him, precisely because he did not intervene on the occasion of this censure motion.

H.B.: Were relations with the workers established on your initiative, or by pressure from the base? What do you think was the meaning of these links?

J.S.: We have long felt the need for this unity. Contacts with

[1] Waldeck-Rochet: General Secretary of the French Communist Party.

the workers were very difficult so long as students were alone in the struggle. But once the battle had spread to the workers, the desire for unity grew quite naturally, both in UNEF and in the mass of students. Relations were opened with the union organizations with a view to a vast discussion at the base, which would decide on its own forms of action and its own aims. We held a joint press conference with the CFDT because it was favourable to the workers becoming aware of the responsibilities owed them; an awareness parallel to the awareness that impelled students in the faculties to take control of their own education.

On the basis of this community of views and our mutual desire to extend discussion at the base, we were able to achieve an alliance, an alliance implying no political or trade-union agreement. All our difficulties with the CGT, on the other hand, derived from the fact that it feared these discussions at the base. But I believe the original agreement was very spontaneous and popular on both sides: remember the welcome given on various occasions to the trade union representatives who came to give their support to the students.

H.B.: You think you have realized the old dream of the students in the Liberation Movement?

J.S.: Yes. Especially among young workers. You know the difficulties we had organizing the march from the Sorbonne to Boulogne-Billancourt, the day after the Renault occupation. When we arrived, I was much struck by the fact that only the young workers came to welcome us. Everyone knows that Boulogne-Billancourt is a CGT fief; the CFDT and the FO are much less well entrenched there.

At present, we should also mention the movements developing inside the youth-clubs and the *Maisons de la Culture*. In

UNEF proposes we said, 'We must extend the struggle to the means of communication, the means of culture.'

H.B.: Student demands seem to be political much more than strictly trade-union demands, whereas those of the workers are primarily social and professional. To what do you attribute this discrepancy?

J.S.: To the influence of the organizations. I believe in mass spontaneity, but also in the necessity for organizations able to make the mass aware that their 'primary' claims presuppose a number of other claims, and lead on to the problem of the regime. So the initial role of union organizations is important, and the fact that the CFDT relatively quickly posed the problem of workers' power greatly favoured factory discussions and the workers' reaction in demanding a popular government. Even the PCF was caught in its own trap, as was the CGT, for the workers were posing the problem of power when they made their material demands. The realization grew among the workers that they would only be able to hang on to the fruits of their few victories if they could acquire some power within their factories. For example, the concrete problem of working hours lost in strikes: the government refuses to treat them wholly as unemployed hours, and only then with loss of bonuses. What they have obtained is already threatened straightaway, if they have no coercive power.

On the other hand, the workers want to express themselves, but they have no means of making themselves heard. On the political level, they have no representatives to express their point of view. They have realized that the government is not an interlocutor and cannot answer to their aspirations, and that the deputies do not represent them. That is why we attended extremely interesting meetings in factories and elsewhere where men met, regrouped, organized, took decisions

T—B

and carried them out. The importance of the student movement was that it showed that the government would give way before a strongly held position. Then the movement developed in the factories as the workers had understood that they could change their situation.

H.B.: Don't you think the worker-student alliance is open to one permanent weakness: the conditions of workers and students are different? The students are largely drawn from the bourgeoisie; and their situation is a temporary one.

J.S.: The students' role was that of a detonator, posing the problem of power very early because it was forced to confront it, enabling a number of unpoliticized students to take a political stand. Later on, the movement spread to the workers as a whole and the university problem took second place or, rather, it was integrated in a common struggle.

Now the student movement is closely dependent on the workers' movement. If the latter stops, ours is condemned, for it will find itself isolated against a brutal repression, for students cannot engage in political struggle alone.

H.B.: If a 'popular government' were formed, controlled by the CGT and the PCF, who do at present represent the majority of the working class, what would your situation be?

J.S.: I do not see the problem at all as you do. I think the situation must be analysed politically and strategically. The latter is particularly difficult because it is impossible to predict the future strength of a spontaneous movement at any moment. The attitude of the CGT and the PCF has been very hesitant. These organizations, like the Federation, are now going through painful discussions, and it is impossible to predict the outcome. If the movement stops, it is true that the traditional left forces may be able to sweep the board and act as an alternative to the Gaullist regime. But if it continues to grow, there may be a total reorganization of the game, as there was in 1789, when, once the traditional representatives had been discredited, entirely new modes of representation had to be found.

H.B.: Strictly student problems have little space in your proposals. You were given a mandate by students to represent them in their demands, yet in fact you deal with problems in the wider field of major political strategy. Doesn't this transition divert you from your real responsibilities?

J.S.: At the present time, the problems posed are political ones and they include the problem of the regime. As trade union leaders we have to take certain options. UNEF is charged with the defence of students and their professional training. So it is indeed a students' union. But I believe that given the realities of the student situation UNEF is primarily a movement of progressive youth.

H.B.: To come to your political options, what do you understand by revolutionary power?

J.S.: The population is a prey to certain fears. It now wants to pose clearly certain simple problems. It is offered various 'gimmicks', the Mitterrand 'gimmick', the Mendès-France 'gimmick', and wonders which of the two would be the more effective. But what is more serious, the population is organized, in factories, in cities and in universities. Some faculties are already functioning under student power. It is our slogan. We are not proposing one 'gimmick' in exchange for another, but a different kind of conception of society: we must prove in action that workers can make their factories work.

The population and the workers must be reassured. We must propose to them, not another government, but the effective power of the workers in their factories. They must be the ones to decide. They are not yet completely organized, but when they are the problem will have been solved. Look at the action committees in the *quartiers* where discussion and organization is taking place. This might well give rise to a new type of management.

H.B.: What does workers' control mean to you?

J.S.: The control of firms by the workers. Power to the workers.

H.B.: In other words, non-authoritarian socialism. Is this derived from any examples? This is the first time that the expression has appeared in France.

J.S.: We no longer speak of 'soviets' because the word is old-fashioned. But that is what we are really talking about when we refer to workers' control.

H.B.: It seems fairly close to the line of French libertarian socialism.

J.S.: Exactly. It is a heritage of the French revolutions of the nineteenth century.

H.B.: Can you tell me what you mean by 'student power'? Aren't you afraid that this student power cuts you off from 'academic power', the power of university teachers, and leads them to consolidate the mandarin positions that some of them have?

J.S.: The formula 'student power' is an ambiguous one. It must be defined in relation to 'workers' power': the factory to the workers, the university to the students. We do not regard student power as co-determination, which we don't believe in, nor as equal representation. Student power is manifested by their veto. Whatever the balance of forces, only this right can make student power concrete. Besides, many faculties have already adopted this proposal, and the veto formula has support. We do not see it as essential to run our universities in a capitalist system, but to initiate a permanent challenge, by way of student power. For it is essential that we maintain a permanently 'critical' stand if we are not to be caught in the traps of the organizations.

H.B.: Attracted though I am to the idea of a permanent challenge, the idea of a veto has the air of a blockage, a stalemate, of negative power.

J.S.: We are not concerned with the formula, the expression. We are concerned with its content: the permanent challenge. Thus, where the balance of forces is in our favour, we can take over the university and push forward a new conception. Where the balance of forces is unfavourable, we shall not participate according to the co-determination model. What we are aiming for is a number of parallel structures that will begin a dialectical movement. If you find the word 'veto' too negative, you can find another.

H.B.: Don't you think you might be sandwiched between this hierarchy and the political authorities? Wouldn't it be more profitable to unite with the academic body, which is of some account, and which could become a power in conjunction with the working masses?

J.S.: If there must be academic power, and a division of responsibilities, decision-making must combine students and
teachers. And the challenge, as well as the running of the
university, must be held in common between these three
categories: students, teachers, administrative staff. Do we want
to oppose students and teachers? That is a false problem. It is
also typical that it should be *La Nation* that declares, 'It is
true, we must recognize that there is an educational crisis;
there are pedagogic problems between students and teachers.'

These problems still have to be solved, but they are not
essential. Besides, at the moment there are a number of teachers who have chosen, and this choice has produced a division.
There is bound to be a split in the teaching body as well as in
the students. That is the only way to avoid the 'sandwiching'
you talked about. Lastly, we should not underestimate the
importance of one of the teachers' unions, which is fighting
at our side: SNESup.

H.B.: Among the activists in the movement, particularly in
the provinces, there are some who say that the problem has
not been correctly posed, and even seems secondary beside
that of the massive influx of young workers into the universities; that then all the problems will be posed in a different
way, in a democratic perspective, and that in fact the phenomenon of the redistribution of power in the teaching body
and the university more generally is relatively unimportant.

J.S.: The facts show that the problem of university power was
important. It was precisely because the workers heard that the
problem of power could be posed that they posed it themselves in the factories. The problem of the availability of
education and its democratization exists too. But is it really
working in a socialist perspective to train a number of cadres
even sons of workers, to exploit the rest of the workers? For

today the university trains cadres[1] who participate in one way or another in the maintenance of the capitalist system, especially by becoming society's watch-dogs, spreading the ideology of the ruling class. Which does not mean that they are not victims of this society too.

The problem of the revolt of the cadres is a real, but ambiguous one. They have realized that power is slipping away from them as a consequence of its greater and greater concentration. It remains to be seen how these same cadres mean to share this power with the working class.

To pose the problem of the availability of education to workers' children as a pre-condition is a false move. The problem is a real one, because everyone has a right to a skill, but it is distorted in the present system. So, in UNEF, we think that the problem of democratization should be posed conjointly with that of the structures of higher education and the socio-economic environment of that education.

H.B.: How can you create a new, socialist university in a capitalist society? Isn't that contradictory?

J.S.: Of course it is. It brings the aims and content of education into question. And even where the democratization of education is concerned we should have no illusions. If few workers' or peasants' children can get into university it is not just because of the barriers to higher education, it is because from childhood they have become accustomed to a kind of thought that prevents them finding a place in the educational system and making their career there on the same basis as the others. So the problem arises even in the infant school. Once the sixth form is reached, most of the children of workers and peasants have been eliminated. So we must struggle with society and thereby redefine the goals of education.

[1] Cadres are the administrators.

To return to your question, a socialist university cannot grow up in a capitalist society. A university has a number of functions which are themselves linked to a particular system. So, in a capitalist society, it is impossible to have a university that functions for the workers. In these circumstances, our job is to turn as much light as possible on to the contradictions within the university system and in society; thus it will be possible to develop a dialectical movement that allows the growth of consciousness among students and among the population as a whole.

So we must set up a number of challenging powers, parallel structures, and confront the problems of the capitalist university, with the aim of destroying that university. The situation can be made to evolve, given this dialectical, and therefore dynamic, movement.

H.B.: Do you think that a new type of society will be worked out by stages, or will it take the form of a permanent challenge? Does the disorder you are accused of have a political content? Is the abolition of political, social and cultural constraints and myths a necessary pre-condition, or do you regard it as an end in itself? What action methods and groupings do you propose?

J.S.: I believe that the creation of a new kind of society by stages is a myth, and one on which several political parties depend. The necessity for a transitional period is another thing. Obviously, we cannot pass from one society to another overnight. At present we are, in fact, in a transitional period, thanks to our permanent challenge, though perhaps not yet at the political level.

It seems to me that it would be wrong to discuss the problem of someone like Mendès-France. The question is, will he participate in the movement or not? The same goes for the others . . . It is true that we have created a certain amount of disorder, but this disorder has had some positive aspects. The students have been forced to think, they have taken a number of decisions and many new ideas have emerged; the same is true of the workers, of the staff of the ORTF, and of artists. Journalists who were unable to express themselves freely have united to find outlets. As to the 'juvenile delinquents', if they turn to violence before anyone else, it is because society gives them no alternative.

The positive aspect of this disorder is the emergence of consciousness followed by action. At present we are feeling a great wind blowing; it may be disorderly, but it is creative, and contagious.

As to the political, social and cultural mythology, I believe that all myths should be abolished, as they distort reality. That is why we want our challenging power to be permanent, carrying on after the movement has finished, as well as accompanying it. Criticism and the abolition of mythology go hand in hand. Before advocating methods of action and groupings, we must first recognize that people are no longer satisfied with the traditional system of representation – either political representation or trade-union representation.

As far as UNEF is concerned, I think that so long as it tries to be a meeting-place for all progressive students, whatever their differences, it will have a part to play. All students should be active within UNEF, so as to make it the organization of revolutionary students. There must be an organization within which the different tendencies can express themselves, and today, more than ever before, this is UNEF's task.

At the moment there are various forms of action committee, some linked to organizations, others without links to any particular organization. Both are essential to the development of the movement. Whatever they are, they unite a number of individuals with a desire to act, and they are important precisely because they have no precise aims. Obviously, they must have a political line, but what matters most is that they should be an original form of expression. Finally, they should spread throughout France and not remain restricted to Paris. A purely Parisian revolution can only fail.

When should we look forward to the co-ordination of these committees? Firstly, they are not yet sufficiently developed. The point at which they become structured is not very important. What is, is their spontaneity and energy. They must not be caught up in an organization that will strangle them. At present we can envisage a skeleton organization that preserves the energy of each action committee. And from then on we can foresee a progressively tighter organization.

H.B.: Since your struggle goes beyond the context of the university in France to include society as a whole, does it also go on to include the anti-imperialist struggle and solidarity with 'the wretched of the earth'?

J.S.: The factory struggle has an international character; capitalist countries are linked together, as are all movements directed against them. The student movement itself is international. We are not content to express solidarity with the struggles pursued in such and such a country, we carry the same struggle to every country.

I don't think our struggle leads on to the anti-imperialist struggle, at the moment it is rather inscribed within that struggle. Among students there is a great sensitivity to the imperialist character of capitalism, and many support Latin American and Third World movements. They take part in struggles against imperialism, particularly American imperialism, sometimes to the extent of forgetting to struggle against capitalism in their own country. But this struggle against imperialism awakens their consciousness. Thus we can think of the present movement as a consequence of the anti-imperialist struggle. Our solidarity with struggles in the Third World cannot be over-emphasized.

THREE

Alain Geismar
SNESup

*This is the first time
that there has been a . . . struggle
on this scale in an economically
advanced country*

HERVÉ BOURGES: What are the general, long-term causes behind the students' revolt? What made SNESup commit itself so intensively to the students' cause?

ALAIN GEISMAR: For several years we have been saying that there is a profound crisis in the universities. It has various underlying causes, in particular the maladaptation of the university structure to its economic and social functions, in research as well as in education and hence in the training of cadres. We estimated that this crisis was not an isolated one but betrayed a malfunction in the social system.

Our proof? Seventy per cent of those who attend university in France fail to complete their courses and, even among those that do graduate, there is an absolutely astonishing number of unemployed. As for the internal organization of the university, it is completely inadequate to an advanced country, with its compartmentalization of the various disciplines, its retention of a grading system dating from Auguste Comte and of faculty structures inherited from the Empire. A number of elements whose main role was revelatory but which are important none the less could be added to the list: the financial crisis, the crisis of resources, and the reduction in the rate of growth – this year once again, we have seen the rate of growth of higher education reduced to a half of what it was in previous years. Saturation point has been reached in the material effort which the State is prepared to put in to adapt and rationalize the university according to its own norms, in the context of the integration of the French economy into the Common Market.

As for the attempt at renovation and rationalization proposed by the regime under the name of the Fouchet Plan, it has essentially two aspects, but they are closely enough linked together to give rise to a dangerous confusion, I feel: on the one hand, an attempt to renew the curriculum, which could not be more desirable or desired, but at the same time, the installation of a university structure adapted to the short-term growth-needs of giant firms, able to manufacture middle cadres via the IUTs, while holding open a kind of noble, royal road for the training of research workers, in so far as the regime would like to compete in the same class as the American system.

This search for rationality within the framework of a changing economy has no social equivalent, or, more exactly, it takes on an anti-social character, in so far as this renewal of the university has not been accompanied by any change in the relations between teachers and taught, not any broadening of the social strata with access to higher education. In the context of the rapid changes associated with the scientific revolution, this is bound up with the fact that scientific research, one of the university's essential functions, has become a productive force, capable of altering the production apparatus itself, and, in consequence, the very situation of producers within the economic and social system; all this is expressed by an extreme tension, and, as we have insisted for a long time, in this situation the slightest spark may lead to a university explosion.

I should like to remind you of the conclusion of a report I delivered to the plenary session of the Amiens conference[1] before Peyrefitte,[2] when he was still the minister: 'Educational renewal can never be achieved by "gimmicks"; it will emerge either as profound changes in orientation, statutory curricula, decreed facilities and university structure, or as strikes and street demonstrations.' I said this more than two months ago, and it can be found in even earlier SNESup statements.

We did not foresee the extent of the crisis, we are not prophets, but we did know that there was a crisis and that it would break out, violently shaking the university and – why not? – our society also. I could add that the scale of the events was due to unlikely errors on the government's part, to the police repression, which released an irreversible mechanism. Chronologically, as everyone knows, the struggle began at Nanterre, precisely over the Fouchet Plan, because the students there held a 'wild-cat' strike in September about the methods for comparing the old and the new systems, which encroached on their positions.

This 'wild-cat' strike surprised everyone; there was much talk of a new kind of trade unionism, outside union structures, of a new style, and there was an attempt to canalize these initiatives. The government and the university authorities tried to set up 'communication' structures, equal-representation commissions, and for some time the students played their game. But they soon found that they were restricted by an enormous contradiction: they were authorized to discuss everything but fundamentals, since at the level of the equal-representation commissions, in the restricted context of one discipline in one faculty, it was impossible to question the function of the university as a whole, the object of the

[1] Amiens Conference: Conference about improving teaching.
[2] Alain Peyrefitte: young Minister of Education who resigned on May 28th, 1968.

conflict. Realizing that they had somehow been trapped, they developed deliberately provocative action. And then errors accumulated on the part of the university authorities and the government.

First, Cohn-Bendit and a number of his comrades were brought before the disciplinary board, and the Nanterre faculty was closed on the mere announcement that the 'Occident' group, an almost non-existent fascist 'groupuscule', had attacked the faculty; the Nanterre students then moved on to the Sorbonne for a protest meeting, which was attended by every student leader, whether political or trade-union. The Rector panicked, and, losing all control of the situation, asked for authorization to close the Sorbonne; meanwhile the police entered the Sorbonne with some brutality, and, on the pretext that three chairs had been broken, arrested all the political and trade-union representatives of the student movement.

That was on Friday, May 3rd, at about four o'clock in the afternoon. Half an hour later, every student in the Latin Quarter was facing the police. With no leaders left, a perfectly spontaneous and unexpectedly violent demonstration was crushed with unprecedented brutality. At ten o'clock that evening, before any other organization, before even UNEF whose leaders were 'in prison', those members of the executive of SNESup present issued an order for a general strike in solidarity with the students. We hoped that this solidarity would be as wide as possible, and not only opposed to the repression, but supporting the same struggle. Obviously at that moment we did not agree with all the modalities of this struggle, nor with all the themes proposed. But from that day on, we have reckoned that we could not divide this solidarity, that these students and their methods and aims brought into question the university that we had condemned and that they were victims of repression by the same authorities whom we had been fighting for years.

Such was our initial commitment. What followed is too familiar to dwell on. Demonstration followed demonstration, and each was tougher than the last. At the beginning we supported them without participating directly; then we declared that if the demonstrations had become so bloody and violent, the teacher's place was beside his students, even in the streets, and a new phase began. If I may say so, we were pleased to find that we were very generally followed by the teaching body in higher education. Day by day the teachers grew in number.

As the repression increased, a reflex solidarity (initially a sentimental one) grew among the working class, for its traditions are such that when the police beat other people, the workers imagine themselves beside those being massacred; later on, the workers realized that the authorities could be made to retreat a certain distance, and to accept the conditions posed by the street demonstrations; and this realization, along with very deep social unrest, spread and broadened into an open struggle. Then followed the factory occupations, which were spontaneous at first, but were later supported and organized by the workers' federations.

H.B.: As you have said, many teachers associated themselves with the student movement. But some kept their distance, and others went to the opposite extreme, even though they were known to be more or less opposed to the reforms originally. Don't you think that even today there are serious divergencies, if not antagonisms, between the students, who want to forge ahead, and the teachers, who fear for the future?

A.G.: That is absolutely true. In our union – embracing something like a third of the university teaching body – we have long led a very hard struggle against the academic mandarinate, which we regard as almost as much an enemy as the

49

government, the political regime – and we have been strongly attacked for doing so. We think that if the university structure remains fixed it is not only because it is inserted in modern capitalist society, with its tendencies to monopoly concentration, but also because the academics themselves are largely attached to their privileges, to the conservation and maintenance of the university in its traditional form.

Two theses were opposed to one another, one proposing a struggle on two fronts, the other hoping to unite against the government all those who opposed it – conservatives hostile to all reform as well as partisans of a radical transformation who could not be content with a simple adjustment of the capitalist State. The conservative tendency is still powerful, it has tried, and will try again, to take part in the crisis and its development, both to slow down the academic movement and to incorporate it, thereby limiting the upheaval in the university structure. None the less, I think that the teaching body as a whole is grateful to SNESup for the position it has taken, and the regrouping it has built around the union, allowing them all, perhaps even the conservatives, to avoid condemnation along with the Gaullist authorities.

H.B.: Do you think that this unity will be maintained in the future? Aren't you afraid that it will collapse tomorrow if the government – whatever the regime – were to favour a 'moderate' regrouping, dividing the student movement from the teachers' movement?

A.G.: Despite some resistance, the movement is irreversible. When teachers find themselves on the barricades with their students, relations can never be quite the same again; when universities opt for autonomy, so long as this autonomy has a real content, a breach has been made in the nature of the central authority, its uniformity and rigidity. No doubt there will be splits, among the students as well as the teachers, and I believe that such splits are a healthy, revelatory phenomenon.

Students do not constitute a social class. Teachers, although they are all wage-earners, derive largely from the society that surrounds them, has created them and put them in their places. A number of them are prepared to challenge this society, and although they have been able to demonstrate a certain unity in the face of repression, it is hardly surprising if the perspective of a new university and a new society produces some splits.

H.B.: Other fissures are already beginning to show. Throughout the crisis, three movements – SNESup, the March 22nd Movement and UNEF – presented a common front. It seems that there are now divergencies in their assessments and orientations. How do you judge the situation?

A.G.: It is natural and less serious than it might appear. In the phase of violent action, which is over for the time being, a number of struggles were, in the nature of things, necessarily forced to converge. When the same grenades are being thrown at you, when you all reject the same class university, when you are all in conflict with the same authorities, you don't ask delicate questions in the middle of the struggle. Soon, after the government's mistakes, the power of the State itself was brought into question. From then on it is hardly surprising that such a movement could produce completely different ideas as to how the authorities should be challenged and what structures should replace them at the level of firms, universities and State apparatus, and that these ideas should boil and ferment, confront one another and come into conflict. We, and myself in particular, thought that there was a moment in the challenge to the State power when the union as a union (ours or UNEF – I cannot pass judgment on what happened in UNEF,

51

but I regret that the same ideas were not discussed there) was limited, that it could not claim to represent the teaching body as such, or the students as students, in a struggle whose aim was the overthrow of State power and not just its overthrow but its replacement by something else. Once this power has been challenged, the role of a union must be restricted to the dissemination of ideas about the basic values which we should like to see replace the present ones.

In consequence, many of us in the union – including myself – felt that subsidiary structures other than union ones should come into play, and that the ambiguity between unions and more strictly political movements which can express programmes or ideologies could be avoided precisely by the structures which had been created at the base in the struggle; *quartier* committees and factory committees, instruments made for themselves by themselves by the workers and students. There was no reason to 'cap' them in some way with union structures, which would only canalize this movement and restrict it. At present, the UNEF executive has not made this analysis and still regards itself as a leader of a struggle of all unions, whereas to my mind this is not quite what is really happening. This is one of our basic differences.

As for the March 22nd Movement, the problem is a different one, for it has always had a very ambiguous structure which we shall have occasion to analyse elsewhere, wider and narrower than a union in so far as it includes within it both UNEF militants and militants from political organizations, behind a political line. It is a new structure, which appeared a few months ago at Nanterre and has successfully led a simultaneous struggle on the two fronts without ever being troubled by the ambiguity between them. It represents the students in movement, not the inert ones, which, in my opinion, gives it total representativeness. The latter do not exist in a revolutionary period, only the former count. They are able to take up the role that they have played during this period and also that of political leaders in another phase; their responsibilities are of another kind.

Their struggle has been valuable as an example, for it initiated the development of the other student struggles and then the workers' struggles. They are the source of a new mode of political and union intervention, and, in consequence, they still retain a responsibility of their own at all levels, whereas the union's responsibility is limited to asking questions about society without being equipped to answer them, and to trying to settle a number of other less global, academic or para-academic questions.

H.B.: As you have spoken of a new university and a new society, can I ask you a double question, one to the former Secretary of SNESup, the other to the political militant? What new university? What new society?

A.G.: I believe that the answer will be found as we go along. Perhaps in twenty years, if we succeed in constructing a new society and thereby a new university within it, historians and ideologues will emerge to discover in tracts or pamphlets by philosophers and so on the creative sources of what is about to happen; but at the present time, I believe, these sources are completely informal.

Many people refer to Marcuse. I must say, that to my knowledge, none of the militants in my union, in UNEF or in any other organization, except for perhaps one in a thousand, has ever read a line of this author who is presented to us as the great precursor to the struggles taking place in universities the world over – which is not to reject his influence, for he has apparently been the first to put into writing analyses of a number of social phenomena; we have put them into action.

On the other hand, we are at present facing a major

problem: this is the first time that there has been a revolutionary struggle on this scale in an economically advanced country, integrated into a capitalist system reinforced by the Common Market. We have no reference model. Neither the Soviets, nor the Cubans, the Chinese, the Yugoslavs, the Czechs have ever faced such a situation. If Marxist theoreticians thought in 1905 or 1920, for example, that revolution would develop first of all in advanced countries, no one has ever devoted himself to the construction of a model for this kind of society, so it has to be built as we go. All that can be said is that the relations of production, as well as the cultural relations and the relations of individual to collective, will be different. The novelty of the system is the installation of direct democracy.

Out of curiosity, I have attended several meetings of the March 22nd Movement. It has a number of 'leaders' in the sociological sense of the term, but no 'chiefs', no executive, even less bureaucracy. Anyone in it can speak 'to the four winds'; the meeting does not vote, it sorts out a number of lines of force and any of the movement's militants can express them. A number of them are very well-known, because the press has put them in the headlines and the government stubbornly searches for scapegoats.

It is impossible to tell whether this kind of experiment could be generalized to the scale of society as a whole; but it remains true that the principle of the delegation of powers to an organizational executive, to a deputy or a general council member, has been challenged. Everyone who is commissioned to act as a spokesman for the movement at whatever level is permanently revocable by a meeting at the base at any time. That is new.

On the other hand, the demand for power as it is formulated at the moment seems to me to be different from demands made previously, since, as is constantly repeated, it is all a question of power at the level of the work-place, the factory, a question of a workers' take-over, whether these workers be students, academics, industrial labourers or even peasants. Some even dispute the need for the existence of a State apparatus. This last problem has not yet been decided, and cannot be so at this early stage. What matters today is that the problem of power at work-place level should be posed with such force and acuity among the masses and within a small group of theoreticians and ideologists.

I have been extremely impressed by the dual power structures that have begun to emerge – they seem to me to be symbolic, even if they are not yet spreading – in some factories where work has been resumed by the workers on behalf of the strikers. This is a quite extraordinary phenomenon, which did not occur in the great strikes of 1936 or 1947 in France, nor during most previous revolutions anywhere. It is extremely rare.

H.B.: Where did that happen?

A.G.: It is said to be true of certain factories in Brest, and of a number of big shops in certain towns. Twenty or so examples have been mentioned. Strike committees in Savoy have been reported as issuing bonds for commodities. There have also been rent strikes and tax strikes. The State power has been permanently challenged.

The universities have declared their autonomy and are managing their own affairs themselves, independently of decrees from the national Ministry of Education.

Cohn-Bendit said, 'I shall return to France when I want to'; a few days later he was at the Sorbonne. It appears that there is still a Minister of the Interior, a police force, a customs office. But he was in Germany, he travelled six hundred kilometres through France, and he arrived in the heart of Paris. He was able to hold an hour-long meeting without anything happening to him. Dual power is on its way.

H.B.: So, basically, this is much more than a university crisis, it is a radical challenge to society and the very forms of political life, since you question not only parliamentarianism as it exists at present, but also the principle of universal suffrage . . .

A.G.: . . . of the delegation of powers.

H.B.: How do you see political power tomorrow?

A.G.: I think that in the advanced bourgeois democracies, in France, Italy, Germany, England and Western Europe in general, the right-left oscillation and all its possible or imaginable variations have never been able to give power to any left forces that were anything more than relatively intelligent reformists, men comparatively well equipped to secure a number of reforms, but unable to bring the structure of society itself into question, for the very good reason that they were playing its game, and, as Guy Mollet, I think, said a few years ago, were capitalism's loyal managers: ready to organize it, but opposed to qualitative leaps.

I do not think that it is possible to answer the present claims of the workers while maintaining the system of capitalist profit; they require basic, radical transformations of the social structure, from top to bottom, converting the superstructures as well as the infrastructures. A parliamentary regime with a majority and an opposition, say a left majority and a bourgeois opposition, cannot, in my opinion, impose them, for as soon as the struggle aims at the liquidation of the bourgeois opposition, it is impossible for it to take place within the framework of a parliamentary debate.

The bourgeoisie must be expected to defend itself and the revolutionary power to attack it; this kind of struggle cannot be conducted within a Parliament, it would be an absurdity unparalleled in the context of a revolutionary society. That later on various modes of expression could coexist makes no difference to the fact that during the months and years of social transformation, while the class struggle is practically the bourgeoisie's fight for survival, the honourable member of parliament is an element with no place or meaning.

H.B.: Do you believe in an intensification of the revolutionary struggle?

A.G.: Yes. That is not to rule out certain forms of recuperation, a canalization of the movement. The history of France is enough to show that revolutions have not always profited those who made them. When the bourgeoisie is at bay it may negotiate with the left, with part of the workers' movement, for substitute solutions which as far as it is concerned are merely delaying, blocking tactics, satisfying some material demands but preserving enough of the social structure for it to return to its position of strength at the earliest opportunity.

The modern capitalist economy can integrate a fair number of transformations and reforms because the present social and economic structures are so ill-adapted that the capitalist system itself would benefit by the work of rationalization. The criteria of rationality are not the same. For example, if a Social-Democratic current were to canalize the revolutionary movement, it might tend for a time towards the rationality analogous to the rationality sought by the enlightened bourgeoisie; when finally the balance of forces changed the bourgeoisie could restore itself to power.

Thus, since 1920, every European revolutionary movement has led the bourgeoisie, after various attempts at repression, to hand over the torch to a Social-Democratic system, with the hope of taking it back later on. This is what happened in Russia in 1917 with Kerensky, in Germany with the Berlin

Commune of 1919 and the crushing of Rosa Luxemburg and Karl Liebknecht. Social Democrats were quick to ally themselves with the police and the army in Germany. Similarly in Poland, in Spain, in France in 1934 and 1936, with the creation of the Popular Front. The same process has emerged again recently with the Mitterrand/Mendès-France initiatives, with just a few differences of emphasis and expression.

Everyone knows that Mendès–France is the most intelligent reformist France has ever known, that he can transcend a number of basic contradictions; but he has no desire to effect qualitative structural changes, and cannot do so as a man – without some total change, and that must ultimately be judged in action – because of his *ambiance*, his conception of European construction, the idea of the continuity of economic and social development formulated in all his writings. At the limit, this man who has taken a more left-wing position than anyone else of substance may perhaps represent the bourgeoisie's last chance.

H.B.: How do you explain the attitude of the CGT and the PCF?

A.G.: That is a very complex question. I think that at first the CGT and the PCF considerably underestimated the breadth of the movement; for years they had rejected a real analysis of society and clung to the pre-established schemata of the demands of peaceful coexistence and the maintenance of the global balance of forces. They soon realized the revolutionary dimensions of the struggles that were taking place, but, faithful to the schema, they tried to canalize them, to reduce them to reformist and corporative movements.

The CGT and the PCF would not be prepared to seize power under any circumstances whatsoever, either in France or in any other country in Western Europe, because, as I see it, they do not want to seize it in a revolutionary way, for fear of disturbing the balance of forces. On the contrary, they have long renounced a lone seizure of power, but intend France to play a part within the world capitalist movement. It is a canalization operation. The theory of the seizure of power by the men of the left and Social Democracy is not just a tactical response to the situation, but a profound vocation, a transformation of Communist strategy that dates from 1947, or even from 1933–4.

The PCF hopes for a steady transition to a society whose revenue will be differently distributed, but in my opinion it does not want a very radical or profound transformation of the social and cultural structure as a whole. Look what is happening now in several people's democracies, with the evolution of Rumania and Czechoslovakia towards some kind of social communism.

Since Lenin's famous statement that 'Socialism equals soviets plus electricity', that is, power at the base plus economic development, socialism has maintained the evolution towards economic advance, but accompanied it by a transition of power to the Party bureaucracy, which is something quite different.

If the CGT and the PCF had decided to put themselves at the head of the movement, we should very quickly have had a Mitterrand-style solution, which would have been much more admissible then than it is now. The Party has discredited itself, so have Social Democracy and the FGDS, which does not mean that they won't reach power. But if they do, it will be by some kind of corruption, by a parliamentary putsch or some such electoral operation, and all the forces that have been in motion will be eliminated in its favour. Under its present organization, the PCF has emerged as the anti-communist structure par excellence.

H.B.: Whether the PCF is revolutionary or not, the length of the strike will inevitably produce serious repercussions on the economy which might play into reactionary hands.

A.G.: The workers' demands cannot be satisfied without a profound economic upheaval, an economic crisis. Obviously, when such transfers of economic and social powers are taking place, there can be no continuity. If the social structure is maintained, and the workers satisfied, there is the risk of a crisis. But I think that they could be satisfied without a catastrophe if the economic structure is radically, totally overhauled.

I don't mean by that that we should scrap the *force de frappe*, or find some other trick of the same kind. The *force de frappe* is very costly, but its transformation would be even more costly for a five-year period; that is obvious to any physicist or economist. I mean something quite different: we should scrap the boss and the wage-earner, the notion of profit, and I think that a complete restructuring in this framework would achieve full employment. France is not a country with too many workers; it has badly distributed, badly used and over-exploited workers, quite a different thing.

H.B.: By the liquidation of capitalism, you mean socialism. That is a rather vague concept. What content do you give it?

A.G.: I am not a theoretician. For me, socialism can be defined negatively, with respect to existing structures, by a rejection of all bureaucracy, of all centralized direction, by granting power to the producers at their point of production. Essentially, it is workers' control, though that too is a vague word ... Workers' control and decentralization, the central authority only have a co-ordinating role, not a repressive one.

H.B.: Obviously you're not looking to any foreign example.

But do you think that the workers' control instituted spontaneously in Algeria after independence is an interesting example?

A.G.: All experiments, in Cuba, Algeria, Yugoslavia, Czechoslovakia, Russia and China, are full of interest and rich lessons can certainly be drawn from them. But to my knowledge there is no country with a level of economic, social and cultural advance comparable to France in which such upheavals have occurred. For the moment my confidence in the masses is unlimited; they have set themselves in motion and if they are capable of bringing down one of the most powerful capitalist States in the world, despite its centralized executive powers and vigorous repressive apparatus, I am confident that they will be able to build socialism.

H.B.: But there seems to be a total disjunction between the student challenge, which has gone to the roots, and has intransigently demonstrated, and the workers' challenge. The student demands have become political demands rather than trade-union demands, whereas the workers' demands have remained primarily at the professional and social level and deal with improvements in their living standards. To what do you attribute this disjunction?

A.G.: The disjunction is real and it persists, but it is not so deep as you might think. It is not surprising that the consequences of the challenge to the university were more clearly perceived in the university milieu than elsewhere, as there are no trade-union structures there to mask the phenomenon. I think that the workers' union officers have a very heavy responsibility. But the experiment that the workers' confederations have just tried, their negotiations with the management and the State, has proved to the working class that they could not obtain

61

substantial, irreversible and consistent satisfaction within the framework of this regime.

Once the challenge has been initiated, politicization follows, so long as the State and the management are incapable of giving satisfaction. From then on the struggles are bound to grow. On the other hand, I should like to recall that from the beginning, even if all the demands were not openly disseminated, by loud-hailer, leaflet or poster, the slogans, even those on purely working-class parades, were already highly politicized; after the extraordinary day of 13th May which marked the emergence of students from the university ghetto and workers from the factory ghetto, the blending of those who had fought in the streets and those who had watched their fight, the struggle took on its working-class dimension.

The union leaderships tried to maintain compartmentalization; their whole effort for days was devoted to hindering any fusion (ideological, not material and physical) between those who were already aware of the scale of their struggle and those who were finding it out day by day. A step forward has now been made. Ask any worker at any factory gate and he will tell you that nothing can be done in the present framework, it has to be changed. This does not mean that he has any clear idea of what he would like instead, or that he has no illusions about a Mitterrand/Waldeck–Rochet 'solution'; but his experience is growing daily in the struggle and the latter creates its own dynamic.

It is important to develop this struggle, to structure it politically, at the base where it is pursued, to seek confrontation and discussion. That is how to add fuel to the revolutionary movement. Never try to impose on it a cover of politicians old or new, or trade union leaders; simply allow men to express themselves, something that has been denied them for decades. The workers today are discussing everything: power in the factories, material demands, the nature of communications, State power; and they are even beginning to touch on international questions by way of the Common Market. They wonder why agricultural production enables neither peasants to live nor consumers to eat ... Questions come from every side. Structures of debate and action must be built. That is what has to be done.

H.B.: You talk of action structures, and you have just abandoned your union post to devote yourself entirely to political activity; some people are dreaming of a new and original political movement; projects for it are already being drawn up. Do you have any more precise ideas about this?

A.G.: We do not have to create a movement. It has already emerged with the action of the masses. All that a vanguard of militants perhaps more conscious than the rest might attempt is to facilitate the structuring of this movement, without wishing to manufacture something artificially which the masses might reject as an enterprise foreign to the movement itself. We should simply make the experience possessed by many militants serve the movement, and, although it is very difficult if we are not going to harm the spontaneity, we should try above all to assist in the synthesis of all the experience of debate, discussion and action, concentrating information and redistributing it.

If the workers at Montpellier knew that experiments in workers' control were under way in Brest, the action would advance much more rapidly at Montpellier. In other words, our greatest need is to set up a temporary co-ordination, making comparison possible. I think that it would be a serious and dangerous mistake, which could destroy all the hopes raised by the movement and play into the hands of all the bourgeois and Social-Democratic forces, if we tried to divert the movement into a traditional-style political structure, even one with a new language and touched-up colours.

H.B.: Isn't there a risk that the government will see its peril and outlaw these organizations which it must fear all the more because they escape traditional categories?

A.G.: We already have an authoritarian government. We should challenge the 'outlawing'.

Didn't we launch a strike overnight, without any warning? And on 13th May the same thing was repeated by all State employees and public service workers. Daniel Cohn-Bendit's right of residence was removed; he came back – that was illegal. Barricades were set up in the streets; it seems that wasn't allowed. We forgot to ask for authorization for our demonstrations, and we were told that was forbidden. The bourgeoisie is indeed afraid, and it or Social Democracy will try to use the strongest measures of repression against us. But have they the means? That is the question.

I say, and I profoundly believe, that in face of a general strike movement and an occupation of factories throughout the country, the repressive structures of the State, even of as strong a police-state as the Frence police-state (I am choosing my words carefully; the number per head of the different kinds of police – both uniformed and plain-clothes – in France is probably one of the highest in Europe), the State that was able to break the OAS, for example, this whole apparatus has admitted its powerlessness. Although it would strictly be possible for troops to take over a number of social functions, the CRS cannot substitute itself for skilled workers to make the factories function, students to pass examinations or teachers to teach courses.

They could try killing and massacre but, given the experience of the last few weeks, it is clear that for each escalation of violence by the government, the masses in the movement find a suitable form of response and struggle, before which the authorities are obliged to give way. I do not believe that any other kind of government could go much further without lauching itself into a sort of genocide by firing on the masses of strikers; then there would be an insurrection . . .

In 1947,[1] Jules Moch[2] was able to break a movement by parading two or three para brigades and firing once or twice. But that was an artificial movement created in response to external problems by the PCF, which manipulated a real social crisis from above. Besides, the apparatus was no longer trusted by the masses. The strikes were sectoral and could be broken. But I believe that if Jules Moch were here today he would be no more successful than Christian Fouchet[3] . . .

[1] Events of 1947: Some strikes started at the end of 1946 in post offices, and in April 1947 at Renault. But the major events took place in November and December in the railways, mines and engineering factories. These were very violently repressed. The aims of the strikers were better wages and working conditions, and to try to change French foreign policy.

[2] Jules Moch: Socialist Minister of the Interior in 1947 who led the repression against the workers.

[3] Fouchet: Minister of Education till March 1967 (cf. Fouchet Plan), and then Minister of the Interior during the events of May; fired by Pompidou.

FOUR

Daniel Cohn-Bendit and Jean-Pierre Duteuil
MARCH 22nd MOVEMENT

*The revolutionary nucleus has grown
and tomorrow it will constitute a firm
point of departure*

HERVÉ BOURGES: Would you first of all recall the origins of
the March 22nd Movement, then indicate the number and
quality of its members, and finally tell us your perspectives, if
not your programme, as you have no programme?

MARCH 22ND: I don't think you could really talk of
members. The March 22nd Movement was created for specific
actions in an equally specific context. It is not an organization
that depends on a congress or on a pre-established political
line; up till now its action has been empirical and has associated together all those who participated on March 22nd.

H.B.: How many were there before the student revolt?

MARCH 22ND: On March 22nd itself, when we occupied the
administrative building, there were one hundred and forty-
two, who did not exactly represent 'our' militants, but about
two hundred to two hundred and fifty students who had made
up their minds to move on to action with new forms of
organization, and to sweep aside certain things that had been

67

paralysing the revolutionary student movement for some time.

At the moment, when the March 22nd Movement comes together for a general meeting at Nanterre, the attendance is fairly stable. But the Movement has spread beyond Nanterre and includes a number of comrades in Paris who have become active militants in the Movement. In the provinces we have no militants at the moment (except at Bordeaux). Besides, the March 22nd Movement should not be regarded as a recruiting organization with a national audience. It represents above all the type of action, the form of organization which we have tried to propagate. In the provinces, militants who are not necessarily integrated into the March 22nd Movement have adopted its forms of action.

H.B.: Is your analysis of the basic causes of the student revolt the same as that of Sauvageot and Geismar?

MARCH 22ND: I think the problem should be examined the other way round, looking at the basic causes of the workers' movement and revolt first. The workers' crisis was unleashed by the student movement which was itself no more than a reflection of an acute crisis.

With de Gaulle, capitalism hoped to modernize itself, but it was the working class that was to pay the costs of the operation. Look at the half-million unemployed and the rise in the cost of living. Once the economy had reached a certain level of modernization, education had to be modernized, too; hence the Fouchet Plan and the Fifth Plan.[1] At a particular moment, the petty and middle bourgeoisie had to pay the costs. Education was rationalized to train technocrats. Thus the contradictions of capitalism re-emerged in education.

[1] Fifth Plan: a scheme to perfect the French economy by encouraging the concentration of industry, allowing capital to control salaried workers, and maintaining a pool of unemployed. It also aims to increase considerably the number of people working in distribution.

68

H.B.: What is your present attitude to UNEF?

MARCH 22ND: UNEF is still just an executive with an apparatus, although it has gained a real audience and might still rebuild its movement. We have always attacked it for representing the bourgeoisie; its demands remain within a bourgeois framework, merely aiming at the adaptation of students and education to a system which is still capitalist. Hence its very precise limits. All the actions that have taken place have developed despite it and mostly against it. But as soon as there was a pseudo-mass-movement, UNEF identified itself with it.

H.B.: Why do you call it a 'pseudo-mass-movement'?

MARCH 22ND: Because a student movement which does not include the working class does not represent the masses. It merely represents a social stratum. For the students are also in revolt to preserve the bourgeois privileges that they have momentarily lost in a transformation of society, the transition from competitive capitalism to monopoly capitalism. Hence their initial demands were almost entirely purely corporative ones. Only during the struggle did the students' positions become more radical, because every commitment to action generates a political consciousness. Street fighting leads to political struggle.

H.B.: Throughout the demonstrations, the three movements, SNESup, UNEF and the March 22nd Movement, made common cause. The present explosion has created a new situation. Are we seeing different ways to pursue the same action? Can we still talk of unity?

MARCH 22ND: I do not believe in student unity, for there are

69

no objective interests common to all students. There are the revolutionary students who have broken with their class and then there are the rest.

H.B.: Don't you think that your position plays into the government's hands?

MARCH 22ND: I know that there have never been more than thirty thousand students on the streets. And students are preparing for their examinations, even in the present prerevolutionary situation. Even at Nanterre. The real problem is the problem of the unity of revolutionary students. Only struggle will strengthen it.

H.B.: What are your perspectives at the student level?

MARCH 22ND: The March 22nd Movement has entered a new phase. We have not abandoned purely student demands, but the best way to bring the university into question is to intensify the workers' movement.

H.B.: What echoes have you found in the workers' movement?

MARCH 22ND: We do not seek to include the workers in our movement. We have provoked a revolt, a disgust which acted as a catalyst. A new form of struggle has emerged, a new form of expression.

H.B.: So you want to destroy the capitalist system. How do you hope to succeed?

MARCH 22ND: We shan't succeed on our own; we cannot make a revolution by ourselves.

H.B.: Well, then, how can you talk of a revolutionary situation?

MARCH 22ND: Such a situation is growing every day, and leads us to think that revolution is now possible. Hence we must fix on a date . . . But concrete revolutionary perspectives are more definite that when the movement began. For us, the first step in the establishment of a classless society must be workers' control. When the workers return to work, they will ask, how and for whom shall we return? Couldn't we run the factory without the bosses? Workers' control must be installed to destroy capitalism.

H.B.: Why this primacy of workers' control?

MARCH 22ND: Workers' control, self-management, the words aren't important. But we must prevent a rigid socialism succeeding capitalism. Seizure of responsibility by the workers leaves out centralism, organization, party. State power will not survive for ever.

H.B.: What is your attitude to the legislative elections?

MARCH 22ND: We should not dream of calling on people to vote for anyone. Nor of running an anti-electoral campaign. These elections are a mystification. The struggle will go on with or without elections.

H.B.: What conclusions would you draw from a Gaullist victory?

MARCH 22ND: We have not discussed these problems directly in the March 22nd Movement. My personal viewpoint is that revolutionary strategy should take almost no notice of the votes. Direct action in factory and street is what will change the situation, not electoral majorities.

H.B.: So you define a revolutionary situation as one of violence, or at least of force?

MARCH 22ND: As a relation of forces between classes. Violence is one means of action, but we don't have a cult of violence. However, there are moments when the relation of forces is such that violence becomes a necessity.

H.B.: Despite your distrust of every political system, do you think that a Popular Front government under, say, François Mitterrand, would be a favourable conjuncture?

MARCH 22ND: I don't know. Probably a left-wing government would have an interesting demystifying effect: in a given period, a left-wing government can do no more than any other government, one of a Gaullist type, for example. Capitalism has only one road open to it if it is to survive, the road taken by Gaullist policy, modernizing a number of structures, and Mitterrand could not improve on it.

H.B.: It is said that some students except Mendès-France from the anathema they hurl at the left in general and at Mitterrand in particular. What do you think of him?

MARCH 22ND: Mendès is the left-wing de Gaulle. He has escaped classification, like de Gaulle, who gained power thereby. He is the man who appears to be above parties, above the *mêlée*.

H.B.: You said demystification of the left, didn't you? Might it not also mean a demobilization of the working class?

MARCH 22ND: No. The working class can only be put to sleep by settling their economic problems. And if a left-wing government came to power it wouldn't solve the problems posed by capitalism. A left-wing government would be forced to adopt the aims of monopoly capitalism, and it would have the same problems, but it might be accompanied by possibilities for working-class action and some popular enthusiasm. That is what is happening in England: all the 'wild-cat' strikes there have occurred since Wilson came to power.

H.B.: The living conditions of French workers can't be compared to those of the workers, peasants and unemployed in the underdeveloped countries, who have nothing to lose and everything to gain by a total upheaval in the structure.

MARCH 22ND: I don't understand. If so, why ten million on strike?

H.B.: On strike, yes. But essentially for wage demands.

MARCH 22ND: That is true. But with problems posed within the factory transcending wage demands. The CGT is leading their strike and the workers know they can depend on their union headquarters to defend their material interests. If the majority of the workers follow the CGT, that does not mean that all do so. In so far as a number challenge the union's action, they are questioning the content of the demands.

At the present time, France has about half a million registered and four hundred thousand unregistered unemployed, the latter consisting of young people who have not found any work. It is a country characterized by job-insecurity, in which a forty-five- or forty-six-hour week is the rule. That should help destroy the idea of a well-off working class and an affluent society. Besides, the criterion should not be whether the worker has or has not a television and a car, but the workers' wages as a proportion of the national income.

H.B.: So you think that, ultimately, the perspectives opened by the present developments are a radical transformation and the disappearance of both right and left regimes, and that every political or union formation should expect this?

MARCH 22ND: I think that for the first time there is a chance, a possibility, of a non-catastrophic revolution. I don't say a non-violent one. In my opinion there is no danger of fascism. Fascism today can rely neither on the workers, who are occupying the factories, nor on the peasantry, who are so far advanced as to question capitalism . . . I don't go so far as to say that it is a revolutionary force, but it is not a reserve force for fascism. None the less, there may still be undemocratic moves. Our danger is that the working class will let itself be crushed, that the relation of forces will change, that Gaullism will regain the upper hand and secure itself another decade of power. It might perhaps succeed in modernizing capitalism, and making the economy competitive. And there is another danger: the left may fall completely into the hands of the trade-union bureaucracies, distorting the whole parliamentary struggle.

H.B.: You have criticized the CGT. What do you think of the CFDT's attitude and the solidarity it has shown towards the students?

MARCH 22ND: As far as I am concerned, the CFDT has always been an organ of class-collaboration. Its statutes imply above all the harmony of labour and capital. That is clearly a negation of the class struggle.

However, a number of CFDT militants do recognize that

struggle. They are not affiliated elsewhere because the CGT is Stalinist and the FO even more integrated. So there are honest and worthy militants within the CFDT. At the moment, the action of these militants corresponds to the bureaucratic interests of the CFDT, its anti-Stalinist interests. So it is pretending to be to the left of the CGT in order to gain members from it. In other words, we have no more confidence in the one than in the other.

H.B.: So you question everything that exists today. Suppose the structures are overturned; what ideal society do you propose for the future?

MARCH 22ND: I think a federation of workers' councils, soviets, a classless society, a society where the social division of labour between manual and intellectual workers no longer exists. As to the precise forms of organization, they cannot be defined yet. But there are examples, historical models.

H.B.: How do you see relations between advanced countries and underdeveloped countries in this overhaul of the whole social, political and economic structure?

MARCH 22ND: In the March 22nd Movement, there has never been any monolithism, and often divergencies. Some thought that the revolutionary centre had shifted to the Third World, others that the basic struggle was the class struggle in France and the industrially advanced countries. The time has probably come to return to these arguments again.

H.B.: More concretely, do you think that the Castroite model, although originating from an underdeveloped country, might be utilizable? And if the answer is yes, in what field would it serve as a reference point?

MARCH 22ND: Our opinions about this differ. Some see in the Cuban revolution the model for revolutions in the Third World, and for a society on the road to socialism. Another group, to which I belong, does not think that Castroism is really a model, and believes that Cuba is moving towards a redivision of society into classes. Since the Third World depends on the industrially advanced countries, it is a basic error to believe that the revolution can start there.

In so far as making a revolution means the dispossession of the bourgeoisie and a take-over of the management of the economy by the workers, it is difficult to dispossess the bourgeoisie in countries underdeveloped in the interests of the bourgeoisie in the advanced countries. That is why we have always thought that the revolution could only be made from the advanced countries. Obviously, this is not to condemn Castro or the Cuban regime, but neo-socialism is impossible in a small island off Florida, economically, politically and socially a prisoner. But it should be said that while it has not produced correct theses, Castroism has considerably annoyed American imperialism.

H.B.: Is there any country in the Third World that seems to you to have achieved a successful revolution?

MARCH 22ND: No. Unfortunately, everyone in the March 22nd Movement is agreed on this, that socialism does not really exist in the Third World. We may think that certain countries have made more or less valuable steps in that direction, but such judgments are often subjective ones.

H.B.: Do you pursue your struggle in a strictly French context, or rather in liaison with neighbouring countries, according to a revolutionary strategy?

MARCH 22ND: If the movement that has been launched has

significantly weakened French capitalism, if movements abroad in Italy, Germany and Spain have produced profound upheavals in Europe, they have a common aim. But revolutionary solidarity is not to be found at the level of an exchange of letters. The best revolution consists in weakening the bourgeoisie in your own country.

H.B.: But there has been talk, in government circles and other places, of subsidies and aid from abroad, and more or less suspicion has fallen on the People's Republic of China, on the CIA and even on Zionism, of helping the revolutionary student movement. Is this true? Do you receive funds from any organization?

MARCH 22ND: *L'Aurore* recently claimed that 'the leaders are anarchists, the money comes from Peking'. We have published the source of all our income. At our general meetings we decided that we should charge for any interviews we gave, so that the source of our funds would be clear. We will not take any money from abroad, from the parties or from extra-party forces.

There are pro-Chinese groups; it would not be surprising if they received assistance from the Chinese Embassy. The pro-Chinese groups' attitude to the March 22nd Movement has been an ambiguous one: initially they denounced it. Then we set up a 'student struggle/workers' struggle' commission, and comrades from the UJCML (Union of Marxist-Leninist Communist Youth) participated in the work of that commission. Finally, when we withdrew from Nanterre, they withdrew from the movement; so they did not participate in the movement itself.

It would not be surprising if the USSR were aiding the PCF, either.

As for us, it does seem that the CIA has been interested

lately: some US newspapers and associations, subsidiaries and agencies of the CIA, have offered us considerable sums; I need not tell you what sort of welcome they received. As to the Zionists, they are no friends of ours. We are opposed to all imperialisms, including Zionist imperialism. We condemn Israel's nationalism and her expansionist claims.

H.B.: Do you think that in France itself you have been supported by left-wing intellectuals?

MARCH 22ND: They have been rather out of things, and that is a good thing; they haven't been able to find a place, they couldn't intervene any more, because they found themselves facing a movement that was prepared to challenge everything, including intellectuals, that progressive students were not accustomed to challenge: Sartre, for example. What influence did he have on the movement? None, not even when he came to speak at the Sorbonne.

H.B.: Do you deny any intellectual affinities, even if, as I suppose, you have no intellectual heroes?

MARCH 22ND: Some people have tried to force Marcuse on us as a mentor; that is a joke. None of us have read Marcuse. Some have read Marx, of course, perhaps Bakunin, and of the moderns, Althusser, Mao, Guevara, Lefebvre. Nearly all the militants of the March 22nd Movement have read Sartre. But no writer could be regarded as the inspiration of the movement.

H.B.: Who, then, are your allies? The new revolutionary party that is being set up?

MARCH 22ND: More than one party is being formed at the

moment. And those who are concocting these new parties are students and intellectuals, and it will lead to a new vanguard party controlling the workers' struggles.

As for us, we have never had any intention of creating a new party, but rather an objective situation that would make self-expression possible at all levels. Now that people are organizing themselves, we are not totally in agreement with what they are aiming at, but neither do we have to join the game: the movement has been launched and every current can express itself freely.

H.B.: So you don't want a movement that coalesces, you leave the doors open. But you do still have a minimum rule: the revolution must come from the base.

MARCH 22ND: Exactly. All groups can express themselves in the student milieu, there can be no question of excluding anyone, that is basic. The climate in the factories is getting just as democratic. In the present situation, trade-union and political propaganda at the factory gates has grown more flexible. This is, of course, a defeat for Stalinism, and it could reach a point of no return. The true revolution gives everyone the means to act. That is what we mean by workers' democracy.

H.B.: But against the organizations of the public authorities, the PCF and perhaps the left, doesn't your fragmentation and rejection of apparatus adversely affect your action?

MARCH 22ND: We don't occupy the same terrain as the Gaullist authorities, the FGDS and the PCF, we don't set one organization against another, but, rather, one type of organization against another type. The *quartier* and factory committees should themselves be the revolutionary forces opposing the authorities. You don't oppose the bourgeoisie by imitating its organizational schemata. Action committees emerged spontaneously everywhere; hence their different names. There are plain action committees, student action committees, workers' action committees, popular action committees, PSU action committees.

The action committees characteristic of the March 22nd Movement were organized slightly differently from the others: at first they only included March 22nd Movement people so that we could co-ordinate with Paris. As individuals we take part in other action committees, for example, the Censier action committee, which is very close to us.

H.B.: Are all these action committees, yours included, co-ordinated now?

MARCH 22ND: Many have tried to co-ordinate them, to top out the movement. From the Sorbonne to Censier, at the moment, a group of people claim to be co-ordinators of the action committees. The March 22nd Movement boycotted a meeting of people like Vigier, Barjonet, and Fourth Internationalists who wanted to build a revolutionary movement; the committees at the base must co-ordinate themselves. Don't let's make a revolutionary party to lead the struggles, uniting personalities who claim to represent the workers.

H.B.: In other words, you do not want to impose revolution, but to maintain its ardour. Raymond Aron has spoken of the student movement as a 'psycho-drama' or a 'pseudo-revolution'.

MARCH 22ND: I don't think anyone in the March 22nd Movement has said that students could make a revolution; if Aron claims that the students wanted to do so alone he is wrong. His social situation and his political opinions lead him to minimize everything that might constitute a revolutionary force.

H.B.: As a last question, does not the fidelity of the PCF, the unions, the peasants, the petty bourgeoisie and the traditional left to parliamentary democracy prick your conscience? Haven't you overestimated the revolutionary capacity of the base? Won't you soon find yourselves isolated?

MARCH 22ND: The working class has proved its combativity. Not only had it to struggle with the bourgeoisie, but also to sustain the enormous weight of the Stalinist and trade-union bureaucracies. If it can still produce new types of struggle, it will hang on to this gain. The revolutionary nucleus has grown and tomorrow it will constitute a firm point of departure.

Documents

*Round Table
on Radio Luxembourg*
MAY 17TH, 1968
led by Jean Carlier

EXTRACTS

A. Geismar SNESUP
J. Sauvageot UNEF
O. Castro MARCH 22nd MOVEMENT

A definition of the tendencies of the three movements

ALAIN GEISMAR: I am here to represent one of the unions in the National Educational Federation, which includes members of very different opinions. Our union has always pursued several options and does not represent any fraction connected with one of the great French political families. The firm positions it has been led to adopt in the last few days are due to the circumstances. Initially, the teachers realized the significance of the movement, at the union level at first and then more widely. They know that the basic causes of the students' unrest deserve solution. The unemployment among graduates of the faculties of letters and in scientific research proves that university reform is required and therefore also a reform of society in so far as the latter cannot itself ensure a balanced development. Our struggle is the same as the students',

85

naturally with some differences, but never so great as to break our agreement on the necessary action.

Before the events, SNESup had six thousand seven hundred members, twelve hundred of them professors or lecturers, that is, a third of all academics.

JACQUES SAUVAGEOT: As for the students, they are more deeply divided between tendencies than the teachers. UNEF is not the only student union, the government having seen fit to create a rival organization. UNEF could be called the union of progressive and revolutionary students. Even within it there are many tendencies. But at present a regrouping is taking place in action around the proposals put forward by the UNEF executive.

It is hard to assess the exact number of members, but we reckon that, on the basis of the attendance at general meetings, we must represent about seventy thousand students.

O. CASTRO: The March 22nd Movement constitutes a tiny minority in UNEF. It was formed on the basis of a critique of 'sectarianism'. We realized how sterile verbal differences were in relation to the possibilities of common action. We did not undertake anything as a group. During the famous night of March 22nd, we tried to define the framework in which it would be possible for all the 'sects' to participate in a single political activity: the challenge to the university. Initially we represented a number of tendencies. Little by little the members of the sects regrouped into a more radical movement: the March 22nd Movement. Our cohesion is not complete, but our movement is alive.

J.S.: I stress that the number of members we have is much less important to us than the numbers who follow our instructions. If we have seventy thousand members, we have an audience much greater than that, as the events have shown. Thus, even before the events, we were sure that more than half the students recognized themselves as members of UNEF.

What ideal university would you like to see replace the one you want to 'break'?

o.c.: We don't think it possible to define an ideal university. By criticizing what is, we shall finally define the themes of the ideal university. We know that the university is not an entity bearing no relationship to the society in which we live; on the contrary, it is part of it. The university cannot be changed without changing the society which it is adjusted to. Better functioning forms of university in society are realizable: they would be better adjusted universities, not ideal ones.

j.s.: The expression 'ideal university' is a bad one. Extremely concrete proposals on the most varied issues have emerged from the present discussions: on examinations, for example, or, more important, on the structure of the *grandes écoles*. So the problem is not one of reasoning on a utopian basis, but of reasoning as a function of a practical situation; it is a question of a critical analysis, and of proposals related to this situation.

The students make two kinds of proposal: those regarding the results at the end of the year; the examinations and the admissions. These problems must be resolved concretely. And then there are those touching on more general problems without ideal solutions at present: what should be the aim of education? What should be the content of studies? The students are trying to lay the foundations for a new university in their current meetings. But you cannot ask them for ready answers, for we are only at the beginning of the constructive phase (what has not been done in ten years can't be done in a few days) and above all because all the basic solutions to academic problems bring the university environment into question.

A.G.: We made a critical analysis of the university situation a long time ago and the theme of our last congress was an attempt to alter a particular university practice. We advanced a number of topics that seemed likely to produce solutions: a critique of the compartmentalization induced by the old faculty structures, from which arose the proposal of interdisciplinary departments; the problem of the lack of outlets for students eliminated during their studies, whence the proposal of diversified structures enabling us to give a professional training; the demand for greater autonomy for establishments of higher education, for a change in staff recruitment in higher education, and for student-teacher commissions. This happened two years ago, and we have still had no response.

We found our way barred by a double wall: a few mandarins rejected any change in the university, while the government sought to rationalize the system without altering it. We regard the present wide debate as very important, and we shall bring up all these discussions again in the battle. But we go further: our graduates find themselves in an impossible situation today, without outlets in the society. On the other hand, we have observed that once students have left the university and become cadres – those of them who can find employment – they are integrated into the social system to the point of no longer offering it any challenge.

O.C.: We are not a union movement. We are not preoccupied solely with problems specific to the university. Rather, with those of society. Only as a result of a calm, reasoned political analysis have we reached the conclusion that the only interesting change is a revolutionary change, one affecting society as a whole. As we are in universities, we fight there, but we know that everything is interconnected. Our critique of the university can only result in a critique of society, hence the necessity to extend our action beyond the university context.

J.S.: I believe that if the action today seems more and more political, it is not just because of the events of the last week. The calling in of the police and the attitudes of the Ministers of Education and the Interior mean that the problems have been posed in political terms. Education is going to be of crucial importance for the growth of every economic system today; whether we like it or not, every aim we put forward will lead us into politics. But here I disagree with Castro: within UNEF the political struggle in the university is directed against a particular university policy; of course this struggle is not limited to the university sector, but for us, for UNEF, the academic arena is the principal one, for we are struggling inside the university.

A.G.: So far we have advanced solutions without receiving any response, but at present we think that we are in a position of strength. On the other hand, the experience of the last twenty or thirty years of working-class and trade-union struggle in France proves that if you abandon a position of strength you obtain nothing by negotiation. As to what is taking place in the universities, a number of acts are irreversible: students and teachers have joined on the barricades, and it will be impossible to reverse student participation in the elaboration of the new university structures. We may perhaps have gone very far, but we have never obtained what we asked for by any other means.

The examination problem

A.G.: There are two problems regarding the examinations. The long-term problem of radically questioning the examination system: examinations don't correspond to the real value of the candidates, they falsify a university system based solely on preparation for these examinations, and not on the acquisition of knowledge or methods of thought. On the other hand there is a much more immediate problem, that of bringing the present university year to an end so that everyone does not just forfeit it. We are asking for a postponement.

Since I agreed to tell students on behalf of the teachers that in no case would any student suffer, that some way would be found to assess their knowledge so that a provisional award of degrees would be possible this year, I don't think I have been contradicted. But we should like this provisional structure to constitute the first step towards a definitive one.

J.S.: Our position on examinations is a position of principle, and it has always been clear: we are against the examination system and we regard it as a means of selection and social segregation. Our commissions at present envisage transformations in the mode of assessment of knowledge, in its content and in the methods for its acquisition. As to this year, militants in the movement must not be discriminated against as compared with the rest. The students themselves in the various disciplines should work out the way the examinations can take place.

We also regard as positive the declarations of autonomy currently issued by the universities, even though they might constitute a chance for the government to install what it wants: a system of competing universities. We want to avoid this, so we shall set out our aims in this matter. We are interested in autonomy in so far as it ensures a real promulgation of the decisions taken by teachers and students. We demand: (1) that students should discuss the procedure and award system for degrees; (2) that the content of the tests be changed: no more essays, rather discussion-work in groups; (3) that students should participate in marking and in the final decisions.

What society would you like to see in place of the one you have challenged? A socialist one?

O.C.: The student movement does not interest us. The essential problem is to take up a critical attitude towards the society in which we live. All positions that set out to justify this society are of no interest to us. Our point of view is one that challenges society and its power. We are not interested in transforming the relations of production but in transforming the very notion of economic labour. That means a revolution.

In the eastern countries bourgeois bureaucracy has been replaced by a Communist Party bureaucracy, with the Party posing as the leader of the working class; the problem of power has not been resolved, merely displaced. Part of the March 22nd Movement (another tendency disagrees) wants to challenge not only those exercising power, but the very idea of power, of a hierarchy, a leadership.

J.S.: I am very cautious about this question. What does an unqualified demand for a 'socialist society' mean, given the criticisms we could make of existing socialisms? We should not try to provide a new formula to replace an old one. Rather we should look at reality, which is not a formula but is progressively constructed and created. We want a different society, one in which the exploitation of the workers will cease, and we think that the workers will construct this society in struggle.

A.G.: When I tell you that we dream of a socialist society we shall not have got very far, given the way the word has been misused. The movement will find itself as it goes.

What political movements do you belong to?

A.G.: During the Algerian War, I was a PSU militant, but I left the organization nearly three years ago. At present I and the members of my union executive, with one or two exceptions, are not attached to any political organization.

J.S.: Many students are militants in political parties. But the movement that has developed in the last few days was made outside the political forces and the parliamentary game. In students' eyes, all the current debates at the National Assembly might just as well not be happening.

O.C.: We believe that nothing is healthier than criticism and self-criticism. As the March 22nd Movement, we have raised the following problems: the workers' movement was defeated around 1920, and the promises of Marxism and Leninism were broken. We have drawn three conclusions: that the organization is unable to put its own theory into practice, that the theory itself must be re-examined, and that the society in which these revolutionary movements occurred must itself be transformed. So long as these criticisms are not made, no new perspective is possible.

The problem exists on an organizational level in the factories, or among the students. Every organization should be a provisional one; it is not valuable in itself, but only in respect to the conditions in which it works. We don't want to make the revolution for others: the students know that the workers and the labouring strata of society will make the revolution.

What are your relations with the Communist Party?

A.G.: As a union, we do not have to maintain relations with one political party any more than another. We joined in discussions when the PCF was working out a project for the democratic reform of education; we then said what we thought about it and we published this in our journals. On the other hand, within our union we do have relations with Communist militants who are fairly numerous, but we regard them as union militants, not PCF militants.

The leaders of our union, like many other academics, were deeply disturbed by the position the PCF took at the beginning of this crisis. But we refuse to go over to a senseless anti-Communism. The PCF takes the positions it wants to and we recognize its right to be what it is. But in return we ask it to recognize the right of trade unionists to be trade unionists, anarchists to be anarchists, Troskyists to be Trotskyists, and for them to decide for themselves. That is the only demand we make of the PCF.

o.c.: The PCF as a party is highly logical and it has laid down a strategy which is not our own. We argue with it, without reaching agreement, but the PCF represents a force we must take into account. We are to the left of the PCF: we reckon that conditions have recurred in French capitalist society that could give rise to a revolution.

The PCF's attitude to us is a difficult one; it condemned the militants of the March 22nd Movement as provocateurs and anarchists. Then it realized that the student crisis was a general one and it was obliged to admit its positive aspect. At the moment the problem turns out to be no longer a student problem, but a working-class problem. We reckon that it is not the organizational forces that are best adjusted to reality and can lead the struggle. We are harder and more revolutionary than the Communist leadership. So we would like to be recognized by the PCF as valid interlocutors, a sizeable political force, not as provocateurs.

j.s.: The PCF's position with respect to the student movement seems to me to be a secondary problem. I don't believe that the PCF militants all agreed with the positions the Party took vis-à-vis the students. Personally, I don't regard the PCF as a revolutionary party. But what really matters is the attitude it takes to the events which are about to follow, significant events which are multiplying daily. For the problem of the PCF is the problem of the organization of the working class. So how will the PCF lead the workers' struggles for socialism? That is the only real question.

Will you refuse to enter negotiations with the government?

O.C.: As the March 22nd Movement is a political movement it is only interested in one observation: the authorities are weak when faced with a street confrontation, they retreat before the militants' and demonstrators' determination. Negotiations are no use to us, they do not interest us. The front is no longer in the universities, and we openly admit that we are even to some extent uninterested in universities; we want the experience of the student crisis to be transmitted to the workers.

J.S.: The problem of the future is important, more important than that of negotiation. Negotiations will resolve themselves in so far as students have time to reflect and make proposals; the stake is too great to bargain about it around a table. Proposals will be decided on which will either be the axes of the struggle or the solutions to be obtained. We shall propose a platform publicly. The government can accept as much of it as it wants to. We shall carry on struggling for satisfaction of those demands we have not obtained, on selectivity among other things. We do not need negotiations, bargaining. The government can be no interlocutor for us.

A.G.: We shall stress demands regarding the university. We

shall let the government and public opinion know them. We don't want secret settlements inside committees. We want a public debate. We are not technical advisers to the government, helping it to solve its difficulties. We may be the intermediaries in the debate, but it will take place between the militants occupying the faculties and the workers occupying the factories and the government. And not between their leaders and the government.

There is much talk of amnesties, but we are not asking for a return to the status quo. We want a resolution of the basic problems.

TWO

Daniel Cohn-Bendit
interviewed by Jean-Paul Sartre

*Our action has proved that
popular spontaneity has kept its place
in the social movement*

JEAN-PAUL SARTRE: Within a few days, although no one
called for a general strike, France has been practically paralysed
by work stoppages and factory occupations. And all because
the students took control of the streets in the Latin Quarter.
What is your analysis of the movement you have unleashed?
How far can it go?

DANIEL COHN-BENDIT: It has grown much larger than we
could have foreseen at the start. The aim is now the overthrow
of the regime. But it is not up to us whether or no this is
achieved. If the Communist Party, the CGT and the other
union headquarters shared it there would be no problem; the
regime would fall within a fortnight, as it has no counterthrust
against a trial of strength supported by all working-class
forces.

J.-P.S.: For the moment there is an obvious disproportion
between the massive nature of the strike movement, which
does, indeed, make possible a direct confrontation with the
regime, and the demands the trade unions have presented
which are still limited ones: for wages, work organization,
pensions, etc., etc.

D.C.-B.: There has always been a disjunction in workers' struggles between the strength of the action and the initial demands. But it might be that the success of the action, the dynamism of the movement could alter the nature of the demands progressively. A strike launched for a partial victory may change into a movement for insurrection.

Even so, some of the demands put forward by the workers today are very far-reaching: a real forty-hour week, for example, and at Renault's a minimum wage of a thousand francs per month. The Gaullist regime cannot accept them without a total loss of face and if it holds out, then there will be a confrontation. Suppose the workers hold out too and the regime falls. What will happen then? The left will come to power. Everything will then depend on what it does. If it really changes the system – I must admit I doubt if it will – it will have an audience, and all will be well. But if we have a Wilson-style government, with or without the Communists, which only proposes minor reforms and adjustments, then the extreme left will regain its strength and we shall have to go on posing the real problems of social control, workers' power, and so on.

But we have not reached that stage yet, and it is not at all certain even that the regime will fall.

J.-P.S.: When the situation is a revolutionary one, a movement like your own may not be stopped, but it may be that its impetus will fade. In that case you will have to try to go as far as possible before you come to a halt. What irreversible results do you think the present movement will achieve, supposing that it soon stops?

D.C.-B.: The workers will obtain the satisfaction of a number of material demands, and the moderates in the student movement and the teachers will put through important university reforms. These will not be the radical reforms we should like to see, but we shall still be able to bring some pressure to bear: we shall make particular proposals, and no doubt a few of them will be accepted because they won't dare refuse us everything. That will be some progress, of course, but nothing basic will have changed and we shall continue to challenge the system as a whole.

Besides, I don't believe the revolution is possible overnight like that. I believe that all we can get are successive adjustments of more or less importance, but these adjustments can only be imposed by revolutionary action. That is how the student movement, which, even if it does temporarily lose its energy, will still have achieved an important university reform, can act as an example to many young workers. By using the traditional means of action of the workers' movement – strikes, occupations of the streets and work-places – we have destroyed the first barrier: the myth that 'nothing can be done about the regime'. We have proved that this is not true. And the workers rushed into the breach. Perhaps this time they won't go right to the end. But there will be other explosions later on. What matters is that the effectiveness of revolutionary methods has been proved.

The union of workers and students can only be achieved in the dynamic of action if the students' movement and the workers' movement each sustain their own impetus and converge on one aim. At the moment, naturally and understandably enough, the workers distrust the students.

J.-P.S.: This distrust is not natural, it has been acquired. It did not exist at the beginning of the nineteenth century, and did not appear until after the massacres of June 1848. Before that, republicans – who were intellectuals and petty bourgeois – and workers marched together. This unity has been out of the question ever since, even in the Communist Party, which has always carefully separated workers and intellectuals.

D.C.-B.: But something did happen during the crisis. At Billancourt the workers would not let the students into the factories. But even the fact that students went to Billancourt was new and important. In fact, there were three stages. First, open mistrust, not only in the working-class press, but among the workers themselves. They said, 'Who are all these daddies' boys who have come here to annoy us?' Then, after the street battles, the students' struggle with the police, this feeling disappeared and solidarity was effectively achieved.

Now we are in a third stage: the workers and peasants have entered the struggle in their turn, but they tell us, 'Wait a little, we want to fight our own battles for ourselves!' That is to be expected. Union can only take place later on if the two movements, the students' movement and the workers' movement, maintain their impetus. After fifty years of distrust, I don't think that what is called 'dialogue' is possible. It is not just a matter of talk. We should not expect the workers to welcome us with open arms. Contact will only be made when we are fighting side by side. We might for example set up common revolutionary action groups in which workers and students raise problems and act together. There are places where that will work, and others where it won't.

J.-P.S.: The problem remains the same: adjustments or revolution. As you have said, everything you do by force is recovered positively by the reformists. Thanks to your action, the university will be readjusted, but only within the framework of a bourgeois society.

D.C.-B.: Obviously, but I believe that that is the only way to advance. Take the examinations, for example. There can be no doubt that they will take place. But certainly not in the way they used to. A new formula will be found. And once they take place in an unusual way, an irreversible process of reforms will have been set moving. I don't know how far it will go, and I know it will be a slow process, but it is the only possible strategy.

I am not interested in metaphysics, in looking for ways to 'make the revolution'. As I have said, I think that we are moving towards a perpetually changing society, modified by revolutionary actions at each stage. A radical change in the structure of our society would only be possible, if, for example, a serious economic crisis, the action of a powerful workers' movement, and vigorous student activity suddenly converged. These conditions have not all been realized today. At best we can hope to bring down the government. We must not dream of destroying bourgeois society. That does not mean that there is nothing to be done; on the contrary, we must struggle step by step, on the basis of a global challenge.

I am not really interested in whether there can still be revolutions in advanced capitalist societies, and what we should do to induce them. Everyone has his own theory. Some say: the revolutions of the Third World will bring about a collapse of the capitalist world. Others: only thanks to revolution in the capitalist world can the Third World advance. All these analyses are more or less correct, but, to my mind, of little importance.

Look at what has just happened. Many people spent a long time searching for the best way to set off an explosion among the students. Finally – no one found it – an *objective situation* produced the explosion. There was the authorities' *coup de pouce*, of course – the police occupation of the Sorbonne – but it is clear that that absurd mistake was not the sole source of the movement. The police had already entered Nanterre several months earlier without setting off a chain reaction. This time there was a chain reaction that could not be stopped

– which allows us to analyse the role an active minority can play.

What has happened in the last fortnight is to my mind a refutation of the famous theory of the 'revolutionary vanguard' as the force leading a popular movement. At Nanterre and Paris there was simply an objective situation, arising from what is vaguely called 'student unrest' and from a desire for action on the part of some young people disgusted by the inaction of the ruling classes. Because it was more conscious theoretically and better prepared, the active minority was able to light the fuse and make the breach. But that is all. The others could follow or not. They happened to have followed. But from then on no vanguard, neither the UEC, the JCR nor the Marxist–Leninists, has been able to seize control of the movement. Their militants can participate decisively in the actions, but they have been drowned in the movement. They are to be found on the co-ordination committees, where their role is important, but there has never been any question of one of these vanguards taking a leading position.

This is the essential point. It shows that we must abandon the theory of the 'leading vanguard' and replace it by a much simpler and more honest one of the active minority functioning as a permanent leaven, pushing for action without ever leading it. In fact, though no one will admit it, the Bolshevik Party did not 'lead' the Russian Revolution. It was borne along by the masses. It might have elaborated its theory en route, and pushed the movement in one direction or another, but it did not by itself launch the movement; that was largely spontaneous. In certain objective situations – with the help of an active minority – spontaneity can find its old place in the social movement. Spontaneity makes possible the forward drive, not the orders of a leading group.

J.-P.S.: What many people cannot understand is the fact that you have not tried to work out a programme, or to give your movement a structure. They attack you for trying to 'smash everything' without knowing – or at any rate saying – what you would like to put in place of what you demolish.

D.C.-B.: Naturally! Everyone would be reassured, particularly Pompidou, if we set up a party and announced, 'All these people here are ours now. Here are our aims and this is how we are going to attain them.' They would know who they were dealing with and how to counter them. They would no longer have to face 'anarchy', 'disorder', 'uncontrollable effervescence'.

Our movement's strength is precisely that it is based on an 'uncontrollable' spontaneity, that it gives an impetus without trying to canalize it or use the action it has unleashed to its own profit. There are clearly two solutions open to us today. The first would be to bring together half a dozen people with political experience, ask them to formulate some convincing immediate demands, and say, 'Here is the student movement's position, do what you like with it!' That is the bad solution. The second is to try to give an understanding of the situation not to the totality of the students nor even to the totality of demonstrators, but to a large number of them. To do so we must avoid building an organization immediately, or defining a programme; that would inevitably paralyse us. The movement's only chance is the disorder that lets men speak freely, and that can result in a form of self-organization. For example, we should now give up mass-spectacular meetings and turn to the formation of work and action groups. That is what we are trying to do at Nanterre.

But now that speech has been suddenly freed in Paris, it is essential first of all that people should express themselves. They say confused, vague things and they are often uninteresting things too, for they have been said a hundred times before, but when they have finished, this allows them to ask 'So what?' This is what matters, that the largest possible number of students say 'So what?' Only then can a programme and a structure be discussed. To ask us today, 'What are you going to do about the examinations?' is to wish to drown the fish, to sabotage the movement and interrupt its dynamic. The examinations will take place and we shall make proposals, but give us time. First we must discuss, reflect, seek new formulae. We shall find them. But not today.

J.-P.S.: You have said that the student movement is now on the crest of a wave. But the vacation is coming, and with it a deceleration, probably a retreat. The government will take the opportunity to put through reforms. It will invite students to participate and many will accept, saying either 'Reformism is all we want,' or 'It is only reformism, but it is better than nothing, and we have obtained it by force.' So you will have a transformed university, but the changes may be merely superficial ones, dealing particularly with the development of material facilities, lodgings, university restaurants. These things would make no basic changes in the system. They are demands that the authorities could satisfy without bringing the regime into question. Do you think that you could obtain any 'adjustments' that would really introduce revolutionary elements into the bourgeois university – for example, that would make the education given at the university contradictory to the basic function of the university in the present regime: the training of cadres who are well integrated into the system?

D.C.-B.: First, purely material demands may have a revolutionary content. On university restaurants we have a demand which is basic. We demand their abolition as university restaurants. They must become youth restaurants in which all young people, whether students or not, can eat for one franc forty. No one can reject this demand: if young workers are working during the day, there seems no reason why they should not dine for one franc forty in the evening. Similarly with the *Cités Universitaires*. There are many young workers and apprentices who would rather live away from their parents but who cannot take a room because that would cost them 30,000 francs per month; let us welcome them to the *Cités*, where the rent is from 9,000 to 10,000 francs per month. And let the well-to-do students in law and *sciences-po* go elsewhere.

Basically, I don't think that any reforms the government might make would be enough to demobilize the students. There obviously will be a retreat during the vacation, but they will not 'break' the movement. Some will say, 'We have lost our chance', without any attempt to explain what has happened. Others will say, 'The situation is not yet ripe.' But many militants will realize that we must capitalize on what has just taken place, analyse it theoretically and prepare to resume our action next term. For there will be an explosion then, whatever the government's reforms. And the experience of disorderly, unintentional, authority-provoked action we have just been through will enable us to make any action launched in the autumn more effective. The vacation will enable students to come to terms with the disarray they showed during the fortnight's crisis, and to think about what they want to do and can do.

As to the possibility of making the education given at the university a 'counter-education' manufacturing not well-integrated cadres but revolutionaries, I am afraid that that seems to me a somewhat idealistic hope. Even a reformed bourgeois education will still manufacture bourgeois cadres. People will be caught in the wheels of the system. At best they will become members of a *bien-pensant* left, but objectively they will remain cogs ensuring the functioning of society.

Our aim is to pursue successfully a 'parallel education' which will be technical and ideological. We must launch a university ourselves, on a completely new basis, even if it only lasts a few weeks. We shall call on left-wing and extreme left-wing teachers who are prepared to work with us in seminars and assist us with their knowledge – renouncing their 'professional' status – in the investigations which we shall undertake.

In all faculties we shall open seminars – not lecture courses, obviously – on the problems of the workers' movement, on the use of technology in the interests of man, on the possibilities opened up by automation. And all this not from a theoretical viewpoint (every sociological study today opens with the words 'Technology must be made to serve man's interests'), but by posing concrete problems. Obviously this education will go in the opposite direction to the education provided by the system and the experiment could not last long; the system would quickly react and the movement give way. But what matters is not working out a reform of capitalist society, but launching an experiment that completely breaks with that society, an experiment that will not last, but which allows a glimpse of a possibility: something which is revealed for a moment and then vanishes. But that is enough to prove that that something could exist.

We do not hope to make some kind of socialist university in our society, for we know that the function of the university will stay the same so long as the system is unchanged as a whole. But we believe that there can be moments of rupture in the system's cohesion and that it is possible to profit by them to open breaches in it.

J.-P.S.: That presupposes the permanent existence of an 'anti-institutional' movement preventing the student forces from structuring themselves. In fact, you could attack UNEF for being a trade union, that is, a necessarily sclerosed institution.

D.C.-B.: We attack it primarily for its inability to make any demands because of its forms of organization. Besides, the defence of the students' interests is something very problematic. What are their 'interests'? They do not constitute a class. Workers and peasants form social classes and have objective interests. Their demands are clear and they are addressed to the management and to the government of the bourgeoisie. But the students? Who are their 'oppressors', if not the system as a whole?

J.-P.S.: Indeed, students are not a class. They are defined by age and a relation to knowledge. By definition, a student is someone who must one day cease to be a student in any society, even the society of our dreams.

D.C.-B.: That is precisely what we must change. In the present system, they say: there are those who work and those who study. And we are stuck with a social division of labour, however intelligent. But we can imagine another system where everyone will work at the tasks of production – reduced to a minimum thanks to technical progress – and everyone will still be able to pursue his studies at the same time: the system of simultaneous productive work and study.

Obviously, there would be special cases; very advanced mathematics or medicine cannot be taken up while exercising another activity at the same time. Uniform rules cannot be laid down. But the basic principle must be changed. To start with we must reject the distinction between student and worker.

Of course, all this is not immediately foreseeable, but something has begun and must necessarily keep going.

(Interview published in *Le Nouvel Observateur*, May 20th, 1968)

THREE

UNEF *proposes*

Given the growth of the students' and workers' movement in Paris and the provinces and the results of the first debates in the faculties, the UNEF national executive regards it as its duty today to draw up a preliminary report and to put forward some proposals so as to reinitiate discussion and action in all French universities. One phenomenon, at any rate, is irreversible: the radical challenge to the university is inseparable from a challenge to the established authorities; in other words the struggle has now moved on to the political terrain.

As new perspectives open before the movement that the students unleashed (the occupation of the factories by the workers), we must fight every attempt to slow down the movement, whether by restricting it to purely academic aims or by conceiving the union of workers and students as limited to the Sorbonne courtyard. That is why we must take part in the dynamic movement of social challenge, particularly by advancing the demand-potential where it first emerged, in the universities. It is crucial to propose objectives that correspond to this analysis.

We now have four essential aims to propose to the student movement:

(1) the immediate installation of real student power

in the faculties with the right to veto any decision taken;

(2) conditional on the first point, university and faculty autonomy;

(3) the extension of the struggle to all those sectors that disseminate the ruling ideology, that is, the media;

(4) a real union with workers' and peasants' struggles by posing the problem of the same type of challenge to the authorities in the factory and in professional structures.

These four essential points are necessary conditions for the resolution of other problems (the examinations; selection; political and trade-union freedom in faculties, schools, and elsewhere).

1. *Student Power*

Whether the instrument is a critical university, student-dominated commissions, or a total change in faculty committees, it is crucial that the student movement retain control of all decisions taken in the university. Whatever structures for debate with the base are set up, only a student veto will enable all decisions taken to be put into practice, and prevent integration.

This demand must be put into practice immediately, and it alone justifies continuing the strike.

But we know that this type of power can only be temporary in a capitalist society.

2. *University Autonomy*

Without student power this autonomy is a trap since it amounts to giving power to the mandarins who govern us. On the other hand, without autonomy, student power is a trap, since government and administration would retain considerable means of control. Autonomy means that every decision taken by students in liaison with teachers will be applicable immediately.

3. Extension of the Struggle to every Ideological Sector

The bourgeoisie is trying to drown the movement in the channels of communication, so we must use the same channels, on the contrary, to make our actions known and understood. This means that anything disseminated that plays into the hands of the authorities must be fought: whether on the air (the ORTF and outlying stations) or in the press. No paper must come out if it is printing false news. This action should be carried out in close alliance with journalists and printing workers. Similarly, the Youth Clubs and *Maisons de la Culture*, the theatres and the whole artistic sector should join in the battle for the creation of a new type of popular culture.

4. Liaison of the Workers' and Students' Struggles

The fall of the existing authorities can only be achieved if the workers themselves lead the struggle. This means that the main force for social transformation remains the working class. The workers must take their fate into their own hands and attack the power of the management forthwith. On our part, this presupposes systematic participation in the discussions that take place in the working class, to convey our point of view, not to give lectures. Conversely, every student-controlled university must be open to the workers for every discussion.

Thus clarified, these four points will allow us to act on the situation and realize our other demands:

(i) The boycott of traditional examinations that only serve to eliminate those students who are the victims of an educational failure; a first synthesis of our discussions allows us to formulate the following principles:

(*a*) There can be no question of making students pay for challenging the examination system. This means that they must not lose the benefits of their year, nor must the examinations discriminate against the militants who have been fighting while others stayed quietly at home, nor against wounded students as opposed to healthy ones.

Given that the attack on examinations is linked to a total change in the education system, this means that any discussion on the assessment of knowledge must be subordinate to it. In the present circumstances it is crucial that there is:

student control of any examination procedure or other method of degree allocation;

alteration of the content of possible tests in certain fields;

control of every decision by the students.

(*b*) There can be no question of letting examinations and national competitions take their normal form:

we propose that the CAPES competition be changed into an examination: this means that the pre-established quota of places should be ignored;

on the *baccalauréat*: the *baccalauréat* cannot be allowed to take its traditional form. As a minimum, we propose that school students should have powers of control, and that all candidates should take the oral examination.

(ii) Political and trade-union freedom exists in the faculties. It must be extended to the campuses (under student power with veto), to the *grandes écoles* and to the schools. On this point UNEF not only declares itself in solidarity with the CALs, but also solemnly declares that it will take part in the struggle for the recognition of the CALs in the schools and for their absolute freedom of expression and action.

(iii) No selection at university entrance or for any courses of higher education. Given that a total change of the education system is an absolute priority, we reject any selection whatsoever.

What is to be done immediately?

1. It is crucial to continue basic discussions in all fields and at all levels. But from now on UNEF calls on its militants to seize control of university administration for the students. If discussions with teachers are still necessary, a veto on all decisions is the only valid guarantee.

As a function of the balance of forces, the control to be installed can only be given to the struggle committees, strike committees or action committees which have really led the action in the last fortnight. Where the balance of forces is not so favourable, we must resort to parallel structures (critical universities, etc.) so that we can maintain enough pressure to disrupt the functioning of the traditional university. Though it is applicable in the present circumstances, this line may change according to the evolution of the balance of forces.

2. Proclamation of autonomy must be demanded forthwith. But this proclamation must not be made unless the first point (the veto) has been obtained, with all the necessary guarantees to prevent autonomy leading to a reinforcement of the conservative and technocratic teaching fractions.

3. The battle for communications must be conducted in every university town. This means that no local paper must come out unless it is doing its job correctly and reporting our struggles. Together with the printing workers, we should

T—E

organize demonstrations, occupations of the buildings, distribution boycotts, etc.

In the cultural sector, we and young workers can begin the battle to transform the activities of Youth Clubs and *Maisons de la Culture* into something more combative (occupations, initiation of political discussions, etc.).

In other sectors of cultural life, we can look forward to interventions in alliance with those artists who have taken a stand against bourgeois culture.

4. Occupation of the factories by the workers has already begun. Our role is that of a megaphone in a campaign of political explanation to prevent the government or the reaction cutting off the student struggle from the workers' struggles. So UNEF militants should take part in the meetings and demonstrations decided on by the workers, and we should regard such participation as a priority.

This set of proposals is thrown open to the free discussions that have been going on in the universities for several days.

UNEF National Executive

FOUR

SNESup *explains*

The situation may be described as a stunning demonstration of the fact that the university crisis foreseen and analysed by SNESup over several years is a serious one, and reveals an even more serious crisis in society.

The fact that generally similar conflicts are unfolding in many advanced countries, including the USA, proves that it is not just a matter of the inadequacy of the resources available. But Gaullist policy, both economically, with the work crisis and unemployment among young people, educationally, with the Fouchet Plan, and now politically, with the very brutal police repression, has given the French university crisis specifically explosive traits. They have been the signal for an unprecedented mass movement, and for millions of workers in town and country to enter the struggle with their own specific aims. The conjunction of university struggles and the workers' movement has upset the stability of the regime and posed the question of power.

1. *The Crisis in the French Educational System and the Significance of the Present University Struggles*

(i) THE SCIENTIFIC REVOLUTION

Since the Second World War, the advanced industrial

countries have entered an era of accelerated acquisition of scientific knowledge, characterized by a rapid passage from discovery to application, generating radical changes in entire production processes. Knowledge, research and the training of men of the highest competence have become the motors of economic growth.

Faced by the new industrial revolution, educational systems, based on the accumulation of knowledge and aiming solely at the inculcation of a culture, have admitted that they cannot make the necessary changes. This inadequacy is felt at every level: primary education no longer has any particular goals, secondary education is still content with the schemata of a false and outdated humanism, higher education still refuses to train for anything but research or teaching (and, anyway, it gives teachers no educational training). In different degrees this crisis in the educational system is affecting every industrialized country in Europe, and it is the subject of cabinet meetings and student demonstrations in every major city, from Barcelona to Berlin and Warsaw.

Our masters have realized the importance of these problems, if only recently and partially. The means they have brought to bear on them have not reached the necessary level, and the aim has been to satisfy the demands of this change in production processes at the least expense, while strengthening the use of the educational system as a powerful instrument for integrating the individual into the economic and social system.

The academic policy of the regime must be placed in its international context, notably the peculiar character of Gaullist policies in this area.

Indeed, it is undeniable that at a governmental level as well as in public opinion there is a growing awareness that the USA is trying, perhaps successfully, to use its scientific potential to extend its hegemony over the majority of capitalist countries. This threat is all the more clearly felt because violence is not excluded from the methods employed to maintain and extend the domination of the USA.

But there is a large discrepancy between the regime's intentions and their realization.

(ii) THE CONTRADICTIONS AND FAILURES OF GAULLIST POLICY

On the economic level the failure is obvious: French industry is still backward in most sectors; the rein on production has produced a serious work crisis, unemployment among the young and a lack of outlets for many graduates. Despite its apparent successes in the monetary field, the French economy is badly prepared to stand the competition it must meet not only in the Common Market, but on a global scale. Also, because of the nature of the economic regime and therefore of the social distribution of the national income, it is the workers who pay the price of this competition.

The contradictions and failures of Gaullist policy are now apparent in every field.

As far as education is concerned, the most obvious contradiction is that between the constant growth in the costs of training technically and scientifically skilled workers and the tendency to leave the responsibility for meeting the cost to the individual and his family. The shortage of skilled labour is recognized throughout Europe as an essential obstacle to capitalist growth. The spontaneous logic of the economic structure, which is opposed to any major transfer of resources from the private to the public sector, the consistency of the social structures that preside over selection from the earliest years of education and particularly over entrance to the secondary level, prevent the authorities from satisfying the needs for specialists, in numbers and quality, that it has calculated itself.

Thus capitalism is itself creating a considerable bottleneck in its own advance.

(iii) SPECIALIZATION AND SELECTION: THE FOUCHET PLAN

But the problem is not restricted to the way pupils and students are recruited and the financing of their studies. The authorities need to extend this recruitment to popular strata, and they need to renounce an educational system aiming solely at the inculcation of a cultural heritage. These needs directly question the content and methods of education, particularly of higher education.

Capitalism is conscious of the social danger represented by raising the level of knowledge ('In a period of crisis a well-educated younger generation that is without suitable employment represents not only a dead loss with respect to the investment made, but also a threat to the established order' – Managing Director of Kodak-Pathé in *Humanisme et Entreprise*) and it finds a solution to its difficulties in the narrow specialization of courses which is the basis of the Fouchet reforms, although this specialization is ultimately an obstacle to technical advance; in the maintenance of a hermetic division into an educational system for intellectuals as 'technicians' (the university) and an educational system for intellectuals as 'future leaders' (the *grandes écoles*, the ENA, etc.); in a reinforcement of the character of education as a factor of social integration.

(iv) EDUCATION AS A FACTOR OF SOCIAL INTEGRATION

'Obligatory education to the age of sixteen is certainly intended to act as a substitute for obligatory military service in the preparation of the majority of the population for their entry into the social mill delineated by the ruling class.

'Education is a factor of social integration in its *style*: the traditional teacher-pupil relationship is a prototype of the authoritarian relationship.

'Education is a factor of social integration in its *content*: it transmits modes of conformist thought; the acceptance of established social hierarchies is its corollary.

'Education is a factor of social integration in its *results*: with the exception of a tiny elite, it tends to reduce the choices open to a minimum; this is what is called orientation.

'Education is a factor of social integration in the *people* who run it: the autonomy they benefit from in their profession conceals from them their *dependence* vis-à-vis the social system.' (*Report of the* 'Goals of Education' *Sub-Commission*, B. Herszberg, Amiens Conference)

(v) THE REGIME'S SCIENTIFIC POLICY

The authorities cannot do without academics to organize education and define its curricula, or without research workers to organize and plan research. Whether it uses appointed or partially elected commissions for this is relatively unimportant.)

This power conceded to academics and research workers gives them the illusion that they are, so to speak, the owners of the university institution and of the public research bodies. This integrating operation is highly effective, for to a large extent the teaching body were the authors of the Fouchet reforms, and the academics and research workers elected to the National Committee for Scientific Research (CNRS) make no objections to carrying out the technical preparatory work for the Plan that was expected of them.

We should also consider how much the increasing cost of research and the refusal of private enterprise to take on these costs and the risks involved (even though it is essential to their survival) mean that the authorities depend on public research bodies to carry out their programmes, particularly where research and development is concerned; and what perspectives this situation offers to the unions with responsibilities in the active sector (refusal to let 'major research' be removed from higher education, research in the IUTs, control of applied research bodies – like the CNES and CEA – the role of the National Committee, of the DGRST, credits for military research, contract policy).

2. The Political Importance of the University Crisis and its Extensions

Because universities play a decisive part in the economic development of the advanced countries and in the perpetuation of the existing social regime, the authorities cannot tolerate the growth of political struggles in the university (particularly student struggles) which reveal the contradictions of the educational system and hence the contradictions of the regime as a whole. That is why the government's response to the movement of challenge was to turn to brutal police repression. This repression was held in check and ultimately revealed to the country as a whole the two indissociable sides of the Gaullist regime: reformist when that was sufficient and violently repressive when necessary.

This regime is not and will not be able to tolerate the political struggles and challenges which may, or rather must, develop in sectors as important to a modern society as scientific research, communications and public services, any more than it can in the university. So all these struggles have a considerable political significance as they directly question the Gaullist regime.

But the growth of struggles in these sectors in isolation cannot result in the overthrow of the capitalist regime and the advent of a socialist society. In this respect workers' struggles, particularly in the industrial sector, will be decisive.

CULTURAL REVOLUTION, ECONOMIC REVOLUTION AND POLITICAL REVOLUTION

The university struggle and the mass political struggle that has been grafted on to it have strongly promoted, though not without confusions which still survive, the aspiration for an entirely new society. Socialist in the economic order, it would make it possible to lay the foundations for a cultural revolution: the suppression of authoritarian relations based on a hierarchy of knowledge, alteration of the income hierarchy also based on knowledge. In such a society the surplus wealth derived from social production would be devoted not to the consumption of new commodities that only differ from the old ones in nature and not in function, but to social investments: health, education and art are among the most important of these. The necessity for specialization in work will be replaced by the possibility of learning and exercising several trades in one lifetime, not just in terms of economic needs but by the free choice of the individual.

The movement has also revealed something else that is no less important in the present context: the necessity and also the possibility for forms of political expression allowing general collective intervention and participation. An aspiration for a free and effective political life that ignores the traditional and dogmatic denials, whether they come from trade unions, political parties or any other source, is a basic characteristic of the revolutionary process that began in the universities.

It is also manifest that an offensive action is possible which is based on a critical analysis of the university milieu, a clear orientation that breaks with the traditional defence of the university. It has been proved that when the forces opposed to them are determined and base their action on important contradictions in the social order, the authorities can be forced into retreat or even shaken and threatened. The entry of millions of workers into the struggle posed the question of power. It is a normal duty of trade unions to pose it at all levels, and, as far as SNESup is concerned, at the university level in particular.

The new role of science and the importance of the social

function of education show that the university, the visible detonation point for the recent explosion, remains a decisive though partial component of the unfolding crisis.

So, here as elsewhere, we must use the present position of strength to conquer positions of power that will facilitate the revelation of new contradictions. These positions of power, of course, are threatened with weakening or capture, so they are only temporary ones; they will only be valuable if a militant challenging force uses them as weapons in the struggle against the class university.

3. *The University Orientation of SNESup*

SNESup's university orientation will for the moment be expressed in relation to the following four points:
- university autonomy and the notion of student power, conceived as a power of challenge and control;
- orientation-selection in higher education, examinations and student status;
- the teacher's status in higher education;
- scientific policy.

(i) UNIVERSITY AUTONOMY

SNESup believes that students and teachers should use their present position of strength to conquer power positions within the university system. These positions of power, of course, are threatened with integration or capture, so they are only temporary ones. They are only valuable if militant challenging forces use them as weapons in the struggle against the class university.

Joint control runs the risk of being rapidly enclosed within the limits of a university adapted to the established social regime, hence it is an illusion and even a source of danger if methods for an effective challenge and control are not set up. So SNESup insists on these possibilities of challenge and control by students and teachers rather than on joint control. But we must recognize that at the level of the indispensable challenge, the principal motor of development in the university institution, the students have a privileged role. Autonomy is not a renunciation of the national level planning of education and research.

SNESup rejects the conception of competitive universities acting on their own account, like industrial or commercial firms, as evoked at the Caen conference. To SNESup, autonomy means:

- autonomy in financial matters, within a framework of financing by public authorities;
- free determination of the form and content of education as of the methods for analysing students' capacities;
- the installation of the control procedures already discussed;
- full exercise of union and political freedoms, which implies free communications in university and society.

This conception of autonomy is in contradiction to present planning methods, so once again it necessarily poses the question of the central authorities.

SNESup believes that it is the union's duty to participate fully in the struggles against the vehicles of the ruling ideology whether it be the content of education, the means of communication or cultural bodies. This intervention implies that the discussion should be clearly carried into the university milieu, for the antagonisms are not situated between the State and the university institution; they traverse the university as well as society as a whole.

(ii) ORIENTATION-SELECTION IN HIGHER EDUCATION, EXAMINATIONS AND STUDENT STATUS

SNESup will act against all elimination measures, against overspecialization in all its modalities, for the diversification of courses in rhythm and kind, for the establishment of new courses, notably in technology – hence our demand for the abolition of the *grandes écoles*.

SNESup stresses that the conception of a higher education linked to research must be abandoned unless budgetary dispositions can be secured favouring the expansion of universities and research, particularly by means of a budgetary pool.

However, SNESup recalls that the optimum rate of growth will not allow us to give all students an education linked to research unless we appeal to radically new teaching methods, notably self-education, and the use of skills which also exist outside the traditional university, which again raises the question of the power of assessment.

SNESup radically challenges the traditional modalities of the assessment of capacity, since they express the coercive and authoritarian role of knowledge in our civilization. SNESup will develop forthwith the elements of a short-term and medium-term policy on the assessment of knowledge and degrees. In the short term, no examination should take place without six weeks' warning. The modalities of these examinations and the curricula for them should be jointly fixed by teachers and students in the mixed commissions that have already been set up.

SNESup demands that the socially useful value of students' work and hence its remuneration should be recognized immediately:

– for medical students by the generalization of hospital duties;
– for science students by effective participation in laboratory work;
– for future teachers by pedagogic periods; etc.

(iii) THE TEACHER'S STATUS IN HIGHER EDUCATION

SNESup recalls that it has long since put forward modalities for the recruitment of teachers and for the practice of teaching in perfect conformity with its challenge to the authoritarian relations of the university system, in its IPRES project and its careers project.

As far as teaching is concerned, SNESup believes that a number of new educational advances could be valuable as examples on the social plane, thanks to new teacher-pupil relations, but they can suppress neither the major role in social integration that has fallen to education nor the contradictions of the university institution. Only challenge will enable the teacher to avoid being the docile toy of the social regime that employs him.

(iv) SCIENTIFIC POLICY

SNESup does not have to alter the regime's research policy for the better; its job, along with research workers as a whole, is to contribute to a definition of aims of research which would not only bear a relation to the necessities of scientific development, but would also conform to its challenge of consumption civilization. By its members' intervention in the various bodies that decide on the financing of research, it will try to reveal the contradictions between the scientific aims of the regime and those of a cultural civilization that serves the population and the underdeveloped countries.

4. *The Movement in the University and the Current Struggles in General*

SNESup is perfectly aware that the issue and results of the movement in the universities, in so far as it has brought the regime itself into question, depend on the aims set by the organizations in charge of the workers' struggles.

Many questions must be answered. Will not the gains

derived from the partial satisfaction of the economic demands, fair and important as they were, be rapidly reduced or even destroyed if there is not a change in the economic and social regime? Should we believe that the satisfaction of such demands will bring about an economic crisis and thereby threaten the regime? If so, how can we imagine achieving such a political result if we insist that, except for the abrogation of the ordinances, our aims are all on an economic level; and that on the political level everything can be reduced to electoral processes such as parliamentary elections or referenda.

SNESup asks for answers to these questions particularly from the trade union leaders who are at present engaged in negotiations with the government, because with regard to changes in the universities, although it is true that immediate partial results will make the present structures more bearable by adjusting them, they will leave the more serious university problems unsolved.

It seems doubtful whether the students would have erected barricades for a few more lecture-halls, or that young workers would have joined them for a ten per cent wage increase.

But for all that, SNESup will not renounce the aims it intends to formulate on its own account where the university is concerned; no more does it intend to contain, reject or canalize struggles tending in the same direction, even if their aims go further and their modalities are different from those adopted by the union. SNESup does not intend to give way before repression, and it will not contribute to its justification. The union reaffirms its solidarity with all students and workers in struggle. It denounces the discriminatory political measures of which Daniel Cohn-Bendit in particular has been a victim.

It is not for SNESup to formulate a global political programme; it can only situate itself with respect to those who have formulated such programmes. SNESup does not pretend to lead the students' struggles, nor *a fortiori* those of the workers' movement. But it will continue to express its analyses and aims everywhere.

Paris,
May 27th, 1968   *SNESup National Executive*

FIVE

THE MARCH 22nd MOVEMENT
states its case

1. *Historical*

In the autumn term in 1967 a strike launched outside the traditional political or trade-union framework united ten thousand of the twelve thousand students in the faculty [of Nanterre] on the issue of an improvement in work conditions. Result: the constitution of equal-representation departmental commissions, which soon admitted their sterility.

In the second term a series of sporadic incidents occurred, expressing a diffuse unrest: a demonstration in solidarity with a student threatened with expulsion ended in a clash with police called in by the Dean; brawls in a few courtyards, etc. Also, the action of the residents of the *Cité Universitaire* made possible the abrogation of the internal regulations.

At the end of March a new phase began:

- psychology students boycotted their preliminary examinations;
- four students distributed a pamphlet attacking the teaching and vocation of sociology (*Pourquoi des Sociologues?*);
- *on Friday, March 2nd, after the arrest of six anti-imperialist militants, a protest meeting was called, which*

finally voted to occupy the administration building the same evening. Two hundred and fifty students meeting in the faculty board room discussed a number of political problems until two o'clock in the morning. A day of political discussion on various unrestricted topics was fixed for Friday, March 29th.

The university authorities were disturbed by the turn of events (the intensive preparation for the 29th: leaflets, speeches, inscriptions on the faculty walls and poster campaigns), and set the administrative staff against the students; the internal library was closed and the laboratory technicians went on strike. On Thursday the 28th, Dean Grappin decreed the suspension of lectures and practicals until the following Monday. A meeting of about three hundred students decided to carry on with the next day's activities, but as a day of preparation for the political discussions, which were postponed until April 2nd.

On Friday, March 29th, while a considerable force of police surrounded the campus, five hundred students took part in the opening meeting in the foyer of the *Cité* and then set themselves up as a commission to discuss the agreed topics.

On Monday, April 1st, a majority of the sociology students in the second year of the first cycle decided to boycott their preliminary examinations. They then voted in favour of a text denouncing sociology as an ideology. On the other hand, at the teaching level, dissensions appeared between the liberal departments (social sciences and letters) who favoured the concession of a site, and the reactionary ones (history) who demanded the arrest of the 'ringleaders'.

Tuesday, April 22nd, was a success: the administration could not prevent fifteen hundred people occupying the B1 lecture theatre for the opening meeting, nor could corporatists and fascists prevent the meetings of the commissions in rooms in C Building. The final full meeting, in which eight hundred students and a few lecturers participated, decided to carry on with the movement and to publish this bulletin.

2. *The Nature of the Movement*

The Nanterre movement is *a fully politicized one*. As opposed to the November strike and its 'corporatist' spirit, it has advanced non-union topics such as 'down with police repression'; 'the critical university'; 'the right to political expression and action in the faculty'. By the same token it has revealed its *minority character*, and it is conscious of this fact: several speakers denounced the illusions behind the slogan 'Defend the common interests of all students.' It is clear that at Nanterre many accept higher studies as an initiation into bourgeois affairs. So a nucleus of three hundred 'extremists' emerged, capable of carrying with it one thousand out of the twelve thousand students in the faculty.

The actions pursued accelerated the emergence of consciousness in some individuals: rather than 'provocation' it was a matter of *forcing latent authoritarianism to manifest itself* (cf. the bus-loads of CRS waiting to intervene) by showing *the true face of the proposed 'dialogue'*. Once certain problems appear, dialogue gives way to truncheons. So there was an increase in political consciousness, and also an active participation of all those who until then had been paralysed by the ineffectiveness of the sects and the routine of traditional demands supported by petitions and silent marches. Finally, students and teachers had to separate when the repressive apparatus got moving. It was interesting to see the UEC call for the efficient running of a bourgeois university in which certain 'left' or even 'Marxist' professors were afraid of a challenge to their status in that bourgeois university.

We must insist on the *novelty of the movement launched*, at least in the French context. First of all, *a common labour has been achieved*, transcending the oppositions between sects; we cannot assert their inanity, but a process has been started in which divergence will arise from theoretical and practical confrontation with reality rather than from verbal quarrels between denominations. Already terminological particularisms have been challenged as rigid and unchanged ideas of reality which act as a means to demarcate one sect from another rather than as an instrument of scientific analysis. On the other hand, we were resolved *to avoid falling into the hands of any particular political group or of the administration* and the liberal teachers, adepts at 'dialogue' and conflict behind closed doors (cf. Grappin's proposal).

New issues were raised, in particular *a more direct and effective rejection of the class university, a denunciation of neutral and objective knowledge as of its parcelization, inquiry into the objective place we are destined to occupy in the present division of labour, union with the struggling workers, etc.*

Simultaneously, original forms of action were developed: improvised meetings in the faculty, occupation of rooms to hold our discussions, interventions in lectures, examination boycotts, political posters and banners in the entrance halls, seizure of the public address system hitherto monopolized by the administration, etc.

Lastly, the movement demonstrated its vitality by two additional characteristics: the *multitude of tendencies*, and the *lag of theory behind practice*. The commission reports are an eloquent testimony to the multiplicity of tendencies, and that besides directly political reflections there should be a text on 'culture and creativity' is not something to be despised. As for the lag of theory behind practice, it is enough to recall that no one yet knows exactly what is happening, while talk of 'folklore' and 'anarchist provocation' does not resolve the problem. The 'student struggle' commission will have to face up to the questions: what is the extent of the contradictions induced in the educational sector by monopoly capitalism? what perspectives are opened up, etc?

In the section on perspectives we shall restrict ourselves to tendencies which can be registered at present.

3. Perspectives

As the movement has defined itself primarily in terms which are negative (rejection of institutionalization, sectarian divisions, black lists) and formal (rights of political expression), if it is to work out a line of action it must examine all the problems raised and reflect on their specific causes. While Dean Grappin is satisfied by arguments worthy of *France-Soir* about emotional isolation and the closed academic atmosphere, we believe deeper realities are hidden behind these apparent causes. Can we explain the events by a melange of chance facts: a band of activists inspired by the German SDS, the uncertainty of others as to their careers, the tense atmosphere in departments divided between professors and junior staff, etc.?

So we must go further and try to work out as scientifically as possible the structural factors that lie behind the agitation.

In the immediate future, the movement's continuity will depend on our ability to establish concrete aims for the summer term and for next year. In this area, several tendencies have already emerged as to the conception of a critical university; should we increase direct action in the universities? Should we be more reformist and unite a more significant proportion of the students behind less radical slogans? Or should we reject the idea of a specifically student agitation and give priority to directly supporting the workers? Finally, should we seek to achieve a union between workers' struggles and an autonomous development of our own actions?

On the morrow of the German neo-Nazi assassination

attempt perpetrated against the revolutionary Rudi Dutschke, with the tacit approval of the pro-American German bourgeoisie, we hope that the diffusion of this bulletin will contribute even in a small degree to the growth of student agitation in other faculties so that the criticism of the university can give rise to a radical and permanent political action in the framework of a critical university, as it has done in Germany.

(*Extract from the Bulletin of the* March 22nd Movement, *Nanterre, April 1968*)

Chronology and Abbreviations

Chronology

Friday May 3rd   Called in by the University Rector, the police clear the Sorbonne. Mass demonstration in the Latin Quarter.

Monday 6th   Arrest and conviction of several demonstrators. New incidents in the Latin Quarter.

Tuesday 7th   'We cannot tolerate violence in the streets,' says General de Gaulle.

Wednesday 8th   In the National Assembly, Peyrefitte assures the house that as soon as order is re-established courses can begin again.

Friday 10th   Breakdown of talks between government and students. Rising in the Latin Quarter where barricades are erected, notably in the rue Gay-Lussac. Brutal police response.

Saturday 11th   Trade-union headquarters call for a twenty-four-hour general strike on the 13th, to protest against the repression.

Returning from Afghanistan, Georges Pompidou announces some concessions.

Monday 13th   General strike, parades of workers, students and school pupils, estimated to be about a million strong.

Tuesday 14th   Occupation of the Sud-Aviation plant at Nanterre.
Pompidou announces an amnesty.
The opposition tables a motion of censure.

Wednesday 15th   Extentions of strikes and factory occupations, particularly at Renault.

Thursday 16th   Pompidou announces that 'the government will do its duty' in the face of disorder.

Saturday 18th   General de Gaulle returns hurriedly from Rumania.

Sunday 19th   The President of the Republic declares, '*La réforme, oui; la chienlit, non.*'

Monday 20th   The parliamentary left demands the resignation of the government and general elections.

Tuesday 21st   Debate on the motion of censure in the Assembly.

Wednesday 22nd   The motion receives only 233 votes, and falls.
Demonstrations near the National Assembly and in the Latin Quarter.

The workers' leaders declare their readiness to negotiate with the management and the government.

Thursday 23rd   The Communists call for a rapid agreement on a common programme with their allies on the left.
Worker-student demonstrations in the Latin Quarter.

Friday 24th   General de Gaulle announces a referendum on participation and adds that he will resign if it is rejected.
Student organizations' march at the Gare de Lyon. Barricades erected in several Paris quartiers and in the provinces. A police commissioner is killed at Lyon.

Saturday 25th   The Prime Minister threatens that 'Meetings will be dispersed as vigorously as possible.'

Sunday 26th   The unions, the management and the government negotiate.

Monday 27th   The strikers reject the 'protocol' of the negotiations.
UNEF organizes a meeting at Charléty with CFDT co-operation.

Tuesday 28th   Alain Peyrefitte resigns.

Wednesday 29th   General de Gaulle leaves the Elysée, and visits Germany where he meets Army chiefs.

Pierre Mendès-France declares that he is ready to assume any responsibility conferred on him by 'the united left as a whole'.

Thursday 30th   Returning to Paris early in the afternoon, General de Gaulle makes a speech to the nation on television and radio in which he announces his refusal to withdraw and his decision to dissolve the National Assembly; he appeals to 'civic action' against a 'totalitarian plot'.

Saturday June 1st   Student march from Montparnasse to Austerlitz.

Friday 7th   While in an interview General de Gaulle condemns both the 'decrepitude' of the university and the Communists' attempt to seize power, several groups of students join workers in opposing the police occupation of the Renault factory at Flins. Several dozen of them are arrested.

Monday 10th   A student drowns during a meeting; a UNEF demonstration and clashes with the police take place in the Latin Quarter.

List of abbreviations

CAL *Comité d'action Lycéen.* Action Committee of the Secondary schools, created after the expulsion of a young pupil from his school (Condorcet) because he called for a strike in his class. These action committees fought for the right to express themselves politically inside the schools, and took an active part in the events of May.

CAPES *Certificat d'aptitude professionnel à l'enseignement du second degré*: teacher's diploma, taken after the B.A., for those who want government recognition as teachers.

CEA *Commissariat à l'Énergie Atomique:* Atomic Energy Commission.

CFDT *Confédération Française Démocratique du Travail.* This came into being when the majority of the Catholic Confédération Française des Travailleurs Chrétiens went secular in November 1964. It is a left-wing Social-Democratic trade union, and has links with several left-wing parties (PSU, SFIO, FGDS, etc.).

CGT *Confédération Générale du Travail.* The largest trade union in France (though small by British standards; affiliated to the French Communist Party.

CNES *Centre Nationale d'Études Spatiales*: National Centre for Space Studies.

CRS *Compagnie Républicaine de Sécurité*: riot police formed by Jules Moch in 1947.

DGRST *Direction Générale de la Recherche Scientifique et Technique*: a special commission appointed by the Prime Minister to allocate funds to the research laboratories.

ENA *École Nationale d'Administration*: one of the most renowned schools in France from which most of the members of the government and establishment are recruited.

FGDS *Fédération de la Gauche Démocrate et Socialiste*: a coalition of social-democratic, left-wing and centre groups, popularly supported, and led by François Mitterrand.

FNEF *Fédération Nationale des Étudiants de France*: Union created by the government in 1961. Calling themselves apolitical, they are in fact a right-wing government agency among the students.

FO *Force Ouvrière*: a corporate trade union which limits its objectives to obtaining better wages and working conditions. It counterbalances the two other active unions.

IPRES *Institut de Préparation à la Recherche et à l'Enseignement Supérieur*: SNESup (teachers' union) project to give a three-year course in research and teaching to graduate students.

IUT *Institut Universitaire Technique*: college of technology, created under the Fouchet plan. Its aims are to give only technical instructions in narrow specialized fields.

JCR *Jeunesse Communiste Révolutionnaire*: a student Trotskyist organization whose leaders belong to the Fourth International. They have modernized Trotsky's ideas and made them more flexible. Founded by Alain Krivine in 1966, their ideas have produced militant activists.

OAS *Organisation d'Armée Secrète*: paramilitary organization led by General Salan, formed to keep Algeria French.

ORTF *Office de Radio Télévision Française*: government-controlled radio and television.

PCF *Parti Communiste Français* French Communist Party.

PSU *Parti Socialiste Unifié*: created in 1960 and led until this summer by Pierre Mendès-France, the party is a very small, far-left one, to the left of the French Communist Party. It has attracted young people and intellectuals.

SDS *Studenten Deutsches Sozialistiche*: German Socialist student movement. Issued from a break with the Social-Democratic Party (SPD). They form an extra-parliamentary alternative.

UEC *Union des Étudiants Communistes*: the student organization of the French Communist Party. It was the nucleus of most of the far-left groups. Once powerful, it lost support because of the bureaucracy and politics of the CP, and remains merely a mouthpiece of the party among students.

UNEF *Union Nationale des Étudiants de France*: left-wing union of students which played an important role during the Algerian war. After that its following declined. During the events of May and June, UNEF was an important channel of information, and many students followed its militant line.

The French system of advanced education is divided between the universities and the 'colleges' (Grandes Écoles), both controlled by the State. The system has not changed since Bonaparte. The State and the economy need top administrators who are provided by the 'colleges' where there are small classes and better teaching. Every 'college' has research facilities. The social function of the 'colleges' is to provide an elite.

Every university is divided into faculties, and the teaching there is not as good as in the 'colleges' since the pupil-teacher ratio is infinitely worse.